Ted & Barbara Rogers Life Story

As told by Barbara and Ted
Written by Ted

First Published September 2016
© Fred Waterfall Publications printed 8.12.2016

This Book is dedicated to
Barbara Anne Rogers

My childhood Sweetheart
My wife and mother of my Children
Grandmother and Great Grandmother
But most of all my best friend.

With deepest Love and Affection,
Ted x

All money raised from the sale of this book will go
to
Alzheimer's and Dementia Society

Introduction

From childhood sweethearts, to 63 years of marriage, it would be difficult to remember times when Ted and Barbara weren't together.

Unfortunately in 2010, Barbara's health issues and dementia came to a point where she needed full time nursing came and would have to go into a home. This was one of the worst days of Ted's life.

The nursing staff suggested to Ted that he should note down a few memories and details of Barbara's life and interests so they could get to know about her.

So Ted had to start putting pen to paper, he was no expert at spelling or grammar, as Barbara had always dealt with all the paper work.

But now, with over two hundred pages of A4 note paper full of memories of their life together (and more stories to note down) he's started to get the hang of it.

This book is just the some of the memories of their lives together ——- Andy Robbins

Table of contents

Chapter		page
1	Barbara's Family	11
2	Teds younger days	19
3	Ted and Barbara got married	33
4	Our first car	51
5	First Move	57
6	The Second Move	75
7	Third Move to Pendock	77
8	Interview Portleesh Ireland	83
9	Fourth Move to Markgate	89
10	Fifth Move to Lillington Darrel	93
11	Sixth Move to work with Wally	145
12	Seventh Move Bishops Castle	161
13	Eighth Move Corwen	183
14	Ninth Move to Wetwood	225
15	Tenth Move to Seighford	237

Ted and Barbara on their wedding day
20th December 1952

Left to right —-Walter, Ted's Dad, Kathleen, Ted's sister, Bob, Ted's older brother,
Ted, Barbara, Sheila, Barbara's sister,
George Smith, Barbara's Dad, left (seated) Edith, Ted's Mum, and right (seated) Elsie, Barbara's Mum.

Barbara was born in a village called Lavant near Goodwood race course on the North side of the South Downs. Here she lived with her mother, father and older sister Sheila, my Dad was a dairy man on the farm where we lived.

I used to go round and help milk the cows and on the odd occasion help to deliver a calf, this was always a magical time, Dad always said "this is not a job for a young lady". On leaving school she worked in a grocer's shop and Mum bought me a new bike as it was a long way to travel to work.

Ted was born on the South Downs so they went to different schools, but they were very close together, so this is how they met at an early age. While Barbara enjoyed singing and dancing, Ted was sport mad, I suppose you could say our schools were rivals.

Barbara and her friends used to go and watch Ted play football for a local club, they saw each other from time to time and chatted, but he always had to get back to work on the village farm for as long as he could remember.

A Bit of what went on

From early nineteen thirties, to the mid two thousand and ten, the story of two Sussex folk would end in the West Midlands.

They met on rural Sussex Downs,
And later lived near many towns
Throughout England they worked so hard,
In woodland field and in farm yard.

They later worked with Game,
That's where Ted would make his name,
Whilst Barbara kept the home together,
Feeding all whatever the weather.

Ted would take on many a task,
Both work and social whenever asked,
From ladies football to running fetes,
With help from all of his best mates.

There was always something going on,
With Ted and Barbara's family throng,
Adding grandchildren too many to count,
Increased the family by large amount.

But sadly all things came to an end,
And you will lose a family friend,
So make the most of all your life,
Whether you are mother, sister, gran or wife

Andy Robbins

Chapter 1
Barbara's Little Story
Barbara's Family

Mr and Mrs Smith.
Barbara's mother's maiden name Elsie Hawkins was born in the town of Sandwich, Kent. Like a lot of young girls those days, they were sent away to service, which meant a large country house. In her case it was West Dean House, close to Singleton and Goodwood race track. She was one of many house maids.

Her father, George Smith was a dairy man who worked on a farm called Cucumber Farm, which had a large herd on cows, and was situated close to Singleton on the Midhurst main road.
In the course of time they met, fell in love and were married at the Lavant Church. They eventually had two daughters the eldest Barbara and her sister Sheila.

Sheila belonged to the Girl Guides and got on very well, but she was not as adventurous as her older sister.
George eventually moved to another farm at Lavant, still as a dairy man. Barbara was at the farm almost as much as she was at home. She would often be seen at the side of her Dad hand milking at the age of seven or eight.
She liked to go to Sunday school, liked music and had a very good friend Eileen.
It was not long before hand milking was finished and milking machinery took over, but that did not stop Barbara from still going to the farm and helping with the calves.
One dinner time, her Dad said "I think I'm going to have a cow calving" Barbara said "I'll come with you" her Dad said "I will have to get John off the farm to come and do

the afternoon milking" as he used to help on the odd occasions.

We had the cow in a loose box well, bedded down with straw when the Boss came in, he said, "George, do you think we should get the vet, what do you say Barbara?"

She knew that she used to help her Dad when she could "give us half an hour Boss, I think she's pretty close, Well, I can feel the calf's legs, Dad and the head has started to come". Well, he said "you know what to do slip the cord over each leg and give it a gentle pull". Suddenly out popped the calf, I grabbed a hand full of straw and gave it a good rub. I heard the milking machine shut down, and Dad and I went home a bit late that night.

Chaos on the farm the next morning, my Dad George was called to the office. "I'm afraid we have a problem, a phone call from the main milk depot has reported water in last night's milk", George said, "I want John in here right now". Well, John was found, called to the office and questioned but denied that he knew nothing about it. George said that he had milked that morning and there was no water leaks or anything wrong, also he pointed out that the Boss knew where he and Barbara were the night before.

"George" said the Boss "carry on as normal and I will see you later", John stayed in the office and was given a 'dressing down' after admitting he accidentally spilt a bucket of milk, so topped a churn up with water. Being a single man he gave in his notice.

When pay day came Dad had a pay rise and there was a small envelop for me which I had never had before, and which contained two one pound notes.

Next morning, off we went to school, we were very much into music, Mum paid half a crown a week for me to have lessons at home. Like some other women, she went out potato and fruit picking for a bit of extra money.

Our school was always in competition with another local school, but they were sport minded, and when we competed against each other, there was always a boy who seemed to stand out scoring goals or runs for his school.

It was in those early days my friendship with that special boy really started, whether at school or on the playing field. We used to talk a lot about our families, Ted never liked school but I liked it.

1939-40 The Second World Wor with Germany started, many of the younger men were called up for service, this took a large number of the workforce away, but to fill up the agricultural spaces, the women's land army was formed, better known as The Land Girls. Many of the older men volunteered for the Home Guard, nick name 'Dads Army' but they did a good job.

There was some boys around eleven or twelve able to get a permit issued by the farmer and sign by their headmaster to have half days off to help on the farms too.

The air raids on the big towns and cities was severe, many families and children were sent out to live with other families in the countryside for safety. Both our villages were close to Tangmere aerodrome, so we often watched aeroplanes from Britton and Germany having 'dog fights' in the air.

The war ended in 1945, street parties were held and we flew flags, many American soldiers and airmen went back home.

Dad liked his garden, my sister liked to be a home girl helping Mum cooking or making clothes and bottling preserves, which she sold on the local WI stall.

Mum used to do her shopping in a large grocery shop called 'The Home and Colonial' and it turned out that Ted's Mum and of course his favourite granny also shopped there.

Although never knowing that Ted and I were very friendly, Mum mentioned one day at the shop that I was leaving school. Looking at the manager and his wife who ran the shop between them, his wife quickly responded, "Well, we could do with a young assistant". It was a well-known old fashioned grocery shop, food was still rationed you had to have a book with tokens. After a short discussion with his wife he asked, "What is your daughter name?" I said "Its Barbara Smith" "of course" he said "you are one of our regular customers, I should have known. It's Friday tomorrow, can you bring her in the morning? I'm sure we will have something positive to offer her". ---

Mum had a bath ready for me the night before, this was a long oval tin bath which was kept in an outhouse as private as you could make it. There was no running water, it had to be pumped from the well, in the garden although we did have electric which was run from the farm. The hot water came from the copper boiler and heated by a fire under it and carried out to the bath.

Mum and I caught the bus to Chichester the next morning and went straight to the shop, I was excited to think I was getting my first interview for a job with manager Mr Dobbs. I had to smile when he told me his name. After a few easy questions like 'did I understand the Ration Coupon Book and how it worked?" I said "yes I did" because Mum had always told us how this and that was rationed, and yet there seemed to be a good stock of groceries in the shop.

He eventually came from the back of the shop with his wife "Hello" she said "I'm Beryl, Mr Dobbs' wife" she seemed a very nice lady.

He took over "We have had a chat and we like the way you present yourself, so we would like to offer you the job. You will get to wear a free uniform and to start, your

wages will be £2-10-0d per week, half a day off on Wednesday when we close at twelve o'clock. Saturday we work to 4-30pm and we tidy up before we go home. We open the shop at 9-30 each morning, I'm sure it won't be long before we can improve on those conditions, and you will be working with Beryl to start with and then, when you're coping on your own, at the side of her. We would like you to start next Monday morning, now how does that sound to you, Barbara?"
" Oh thank you very much Mr Dobbs" I blurted out with a smile, he shook Mums hand and mine and thanked her, saying that he looked forward to receiving her continued custom at the shop and will look forward to seeing me on Monday morning at nine o'clock.

We were so pleased, we walked out of the shop and who should be there but my best friend Eileen French. I asked what she was doing there and she replied that she had told me she would come to wish me luck, so I told her that I had got the job and we hugged each other with joy, Eileen had already got a job further down the street.
"Come on girls" Mum said, "We've got another shop to go to, you know Dad and I promised you a new bike". So we were inside with bikes all round us, and I eventually picked one, I asked Eileen if she liked it and she said that she did too. The shop Keeper made sure I could reach the pedals alright.
"You will have something to show Ted when you see him" said Eileen, Mum heard the name 'Ted' mentioned, "Oh, and who is Ted?" she said, I told her he was just a boy that I know. "Well, both of you ride your bikes back home carefully together and I will catch the bus home now" The bike ride home was a three and half mile journey.

When I got home, I gave Dad a kiss and thanked him for the lovely surprise of my new bike, Sheila my sister said "I suppose I will have to catch the bus when I get a job, but that won't be for another year at least will it?".
This boy Ted Rogers, as the days rolled by we got to know each other quite Well, he had joined the local football club, also belonged a Boxing club which his Dad helped to run. He had two brothers who were older than him and a younger sister, he used to do odd jobs at a local village farm where he lived, the time came when we talked about leaving school, although I loved the cows Dad said "it's no job for a young lady".

Mum brought up the question about Ted and who he was, Dad all ears but did not say a word. "I've known him for quite a long time such as school sport days and the odd time when we've all gone together down to the village green. Now he's started playing football for ---p8--- Lavant Club. He told me that he started to work as an apprentice plumber tin smith in the iron mongers shop down the street where we were today. He doesn't like being inside all day, also he's only getting ten shillings a week, he also told me that one day he would like to work on a farm in the village where he lives in West Stoke, which is just over the Downs, "I do want to keep seeing him Mum". "Well, there's no reason why you should not, I hope we will meet this young man one day".
The weekend came and on Saturday Ted played his first full Game, me and my friends and his mates all watched from the side line, while his best friend played in goal. It was a good Game and everyone agreed that a draw was a fair result. The whistle went and Ted came across and held my hand, "Will you wait for me I'm just going to get changed and cleaned up?" "Of course I'll wait" I said.

When I later saw him coming across the field, my friends waved goodbye, Eileen whispered "Good Luck" in my ear. I got my new bike and we walked back to a nearby bench and sat down.
Ted said "I've got some good news for you" "I've got some good news for you too", I said "that's why I got this new bike which Mum and Dad bought for me, because I got the new job I went for, I start on Monday morning" "That's great news" he said and I said "Now tell me your news" "Well, you know how much I like you" so I said "and I like you very much" "So can we say that we are sweethearts?" He gave me a kiss, this was very special, then after while Ted said "You know I did not like that job as a plumber, I could not work inside all the time". Well, two weeks ago on my way home I bumped into a local farmer, who I had always done odd jobs for since I could remember and he remarked that he hadn't seen much of me for a while. Well, I explained to him how I felt and that I had finished there, he asked me if I was sure and I told him yes. "Tell your Mum and Dad I would like to see them later tonight" he said "Mum had already been potato picking for him that day and Dad was already well, known because of his amateur boxing and tree felling over the years.

When Walter, as everyone knew him, came over to the house, he shook Dad's hand and Mum asked him if he would like a cup of tea, he said yes he'd love one. Mr Mason then said that "Ted had told him that he hasn't got a job at the moment but I didn't want to take him away from an apprenticeship" I said that I had already left and Dad said he was not surprised as I always been an outdoor lad. "That's why I would like to offer you a full time job on the farm" said Mr Mason, "because of the odd jobs you have done for me, you know the farm and the workforce

pretty well. There's piece-work and overtime for extra money. I will give you five pounds a week and you can start when you like. Come to the office tomorrow, the secretary will give you a time sheet and set you on. Don't forget we start at seven am, go and see Frank Coombs, he gets the horse ready for then".
"Thank you Mr Mason, that's what I've always wanted"
"Well, I wish you goodnight and I'll be on my way" he said.
Barbara squeezed my hand, we both got what we wanted.

Barbara with her Dad George, Mum Elsie and Sister Sheila

Chapter 2

Ted's Younger Days

The only thing is, we may not see one another quite so much with the amount of work and longer hours I'll be doing. Barbara said "Oh yes we will I promise".

"I think we had better be making tracks for home" knowing her Mum had always been so strict with bringing up both girls. Ted pushed her bike to the little church where the roads parted, she went right and he went straight on.
I will be at the youth club on Wednesday night, see you then. They both promised they would, they kissed once again and parted reluctantly. A quiet voice from the church gate, "you lucky thing" who should it be but Eileen her best friend, "I've been waiting for you", she said with a big smile. I've never been so happy, "and I'm happy for you" said Eileen, they only live two doors away from each other. They both agreed, come on lets go home.

Ted was well, on his way walking home which would take him three quarters of an hour, when he remembered there was a bag of rabbit food which he had picked up and stashed in the hedge the day before, his Dad was also a keen gardener, they had rabbits and chickens and a good vegetable patch which they needed, because Ted had two older brothers and a younger sister.
They lived in a row of six council houses, and of course granny Mitchell lived next door and she had had nine children, his Mum being one of them, Ted being her favourite grandson, all in all we were a pretty close

family.

Most of the Uncles had been in the navy, so his brother Bob the oldest, decided to join the Royal Marines. Dad being an old soldier in the Royal Sussex, served across Europe in 1914-18 war. Ted's other brother joined the merchant Navy being a stoker on the steam ship S S Prague based in Harwich .

With them two being away left me doing most of the small jobs at home, Dad was at work all day, Mum and my sister were in charge of the chickens, I had about twenty five to thirty rabbits in boxes to look after. Dad was also well in with the village squire, he was often called on to go and fell a tree on the small estate that they owned.

Now and again someone from the village called in, have you got a rabbit to sell us for Sunday dinner, Mr Rogers said "go with Ted and he'll pick one out and kill it, and Edith will skin and joint it for you", that was Mums job.

Another little side line I had, I would go up on the Downs to the big chalk pit and dig out some big lumps, wheel the barrow back home, saw them up into small pieces like blocks of soap. Mum after whitening her own door step, started what almost became a front door step competition, to see who could come up with the whitest, a splash of water was all it needed.

Barbara started work on Monday, for some reason Mum went shopping on Thursday instead of Monday, Barbara was serving alongside Beryl. Being a regular customer she went to the counter, "good morning Mr Dobbs" and "Good morning Mrs Rogers". Mum handed her list over, "shall I pack it while you wait", "yes please", and she sat down on one of the three chairs that was purposely put for any customers to rest their legs.

Barbara gave a short gasp, grabbed beryl's arm, she had never met Ted's Mum before but was sure she heard Mrs

Rogers.

"Beryl, may I have a minute to go and talk to that lady", "If it's important, yes, but don't be too long dear". She wasn't too sure what to say, "May I sit down?" "Yes dear".

"Did I hear you say your name Mrs Rogers?" "That's right dear, may I ask why?" "Do you know a young boy called Ted" she laughed, "Yes I should do", I explained what he looked like, "that's my boy".

"Well, I know Ted quite well," "I'm very pleased to have met you, darling, it's for sure I'll be seeing you every week, when I shop, I will put in a good word when I see him tonight", she collected her groceries and said her good byes.

I met up with Eileen and we cycled home together, we chatted and talked about our days' work. It was about a half hour ride, and I had to tell her the whole story. "You never guess who I met today, well, this lady came in to do her shopping, and Mrs Dobbs called her Mrs Rogers". Eileen shrieked "Oh no" nearly falling off her bike, "what did you do?". "She sat down waiting for her groceries to be packed, I just had to go and say something, she was very nice and thanked me for having a chat, and that was it". Ted was so pleased she had met his Mum. It must have been a year gone by, Barbara was well into her work at the shop and very well respected and very quickly received a pay rise.

Ted was busy on the farm which he loved' especially working with the heavy horses, (see picture page 82) working long hours overtime and piece work, but we still managed to see one another as much as we could.

Mum asked me again when we were going to meet this young man, to my surprise on the way home from work, he was waiting for me at the little church after he had played football on Saturday. He rode a rickety old bike, I pulled his leg saying why don't you buy a new one. "No I'm saving all my pennies", little did I know how true that was to become.

"I'll ride with you to your gate", little did I know Mum and Dad would be in the garden. Mum came to the gate, Barbara introduce me to her Mum, "so you're the young man we've heard so much about" "Well, I hope it's not been too bad". "Would you like to come in and have a cup of tea?"

"That's very kind of you but I have got to get back to the farm, it's my turn to get the horses in and feed them and bed them down for the night. I'm sorry Barbara", "Well, I insist you come over about 4 o'clock", she gave me a kiss and said see you tomorrow.

Her Mum said to her after I had gone, "Well, that looked very serious, yes we are, he seems a nice young man, and we will have plenty to talk about tomorrow".

I was a bit late getting home, Mum said

"I've got sandwiches for you. Go and do the horses and you can tell me all your news later". "I told her how I'd met her Mum and they invited me for tea tomorrow".

We had a lovely tea which was mainly from the garden, I said you are as keen as my Dad with your garden, well, it all helps. We talked about the shop where Barbara works, and the farm where I work, especially the horses because there were none where I worked, it was all cattle, ours was a very mixed one.

Her sister came in, "hello Ted have I missed all the gossip", her Mum said rather sharply, "We don't have gossip we talk" "Oh sorry" she said shyly" "Now have your tea and you can help us clear away".

With that done we went into the sitting room, her Dad said "come on Barbara lets have some music". I knew her

Mum paid a half crown a week until her birthday to learn the piano. Her Dad loved to hear her play, the evening simply flew by, her Mum said "I shall go and make us all a drink", I knew it was nearly time for me to leave, we all drank our tea up.

I shook her Mum's hand and thanked her very much, she said "You really must come and see us again", and to my surprise she gave me a little hug at the same time. Barbara came to the gate we said our usual goodbyes, "I'll see you on Wednesday at the youth club".

"Well, surely we must invite her here as soon as you like now you have told me the whole story". We still continued to meet one another, Mum was right, it was time we asked her to come for tea, she was rather thrown in at the deep end.

My eldest brother was home on leave from his camp, but never stayed long, he told Mum he was going to make a home with his girlfriend in Chichester and that was nearly the last we saw him. My other brother who I got on well with, could not get home from his ship for a while. My sister was home helping with the chickens and then getting the tea ready. I rode my rickety old bike to meet Barbara, my way home was under the south side of the Downs. "One day we will walk up that old chalk pit lane, I am sure there is a short cut down the other side to your home."

Ted pushed my new bike with care up the garden path and gently stood it against the fence, she stood and looked around at all the wood that as stacked up, and all the rabbits that were in their boxes. She spotted a big cage a little way up the garden, "is that the ferrets you told me about and how you use them to catch wild rabbits, and are all those chickens yours as well," "Yes they are, and that's the veg patch".

I was almost afraid she was going to run away with fright, she turned to me and said this is fantastic isn't it, Dad was in the middle of the patch, "Hello" and waved his hand, "I'll be with you in a minute". Mum came out into the yard, "Barbara how lovely to see you, I hope he's not boring you", after a short look round and a good chat, Mum said quietly, "I'm ashamed to tell you, that's our toilet over there, we've got no water laid on, but they are getting close. So we are looking forward to having tap water and a toilet in the house soon, we have got electricity at last". "I said thank goodness, no more winding water up from the well." Barbara took Mums hand "don't worry Mrs Rogers we are in the same position at home". Dad came down from the garden, "Walter I think you had better go and get cleaned up", he washed his hands in a bucket of water and dried them on a towel which was always kept outside the back door for that purpose.

He shook my hand "I am very pleased to meet you Barbara, I'll go and get cleaned up properly". Barbara said "What a lovely lawn you have got in the front garden", my sister Kathleen came out at that moment, "Mum can we have a picnic?" "Barbara would you like sit out as well? It's a beautiful day isn't it?" The table is already out there Ted will you fetch the chairs out? It's not quite tea time, and we will go and sit on the bench and have another chat".

"Barbara I am sorry I meant to ask if you like salad", "Oh very much I do" "As you can see it's all home grown". There was a gate to the next garden for access to the well, a voice came over, "Edith have you got enough water", that was Mum's name, "Dad's getting some up, we're out on the lawn" Mum called her to come through "Oh I'm sorry I didn't know you had company" "Well, I think you know our guest" She stood open mouthed, "Its Barbara from the shop, what are you doing here". "Mother, she's Ted's girlfriend" "Oh darling, I'm so sorry, I didn't mean to be rude, Ted you must bring Barbara round before you take her home".

Dad came out and joined in the chat, "Ted, I meant to have told you, you can ditch your old bike, I've found another one for myself so you can have my old one" "Thanks Dad, it's a Rolls Royce compared to my rickety old one."

"I'll be spinning out potatoes in the morning Mum, the others will be out about 8 o'clock, by the time I get the bags and baskets out for you all, Jock and I will very soon have a row out for you". Mum was one of a few women who helped do seasonal work, Jock's one of Ted's favourite horses that he works out. Barbara asked "How many horses have you got on the farm?" "There are eight and two foals if you look across the field there, waiting at the gate to go in the stables for tea". "Yes that's a good idea, it's time we had ours, don't you Mum?" "Barbara, would you like to help Kathleen set the table and I'll bring out the food". And out it came, two big bowls of mixed salad, slices of bread and butter, two plates of meat slices, beef and chicken. It looked absolutely beautiful.

"Barbara, please help yourself", Mum fussed about making everything look just right. As we all about cleared our plates away, Mum disappeared and came out with small plates, and of course one of her special homemade fruit cakes. "Now Barbara you must have a piece of my cake" "It certainly looks good" We tucked into a piece of it, "Would you like another cup of tea Barbara? I know Ted and Dad will have one". "Mrs Rogers. I could not eat or drink another mouthful that was a really lovely tea thank you very much, can I help you wash up? Well, if we all muck in it won't take long will it".

When that was done Kathleen said, "Now I must go and collect the eggs" "Can I come with you?" we took two baskets, "You never know how many you are going to find, there ate twenty boxes to look in, I collect them twice a day". "What do you do with them all?" "Well, our milkman comes round and he'll take all what we don't want.
Ted gets a drop of milk from the farm, the workers are allowed so much every week for free, but we buy the rest of the milkman and he buys our eggs, and some we sell in the village".
We all sat down on the bench, again Mum reminded Ted he had to go and see granny before he took Barbara home, we have all got to go to work in the morning. We had better go in now then, we went through the gate, and Ted knocked on the door, opened it and called out "Hello Granny" "Come in. Barbara, I'm so pleased to see you darling, I do hope you don't think I'm rude I was so surprised to see you. Ted, you should have warned me". "Mrs Mitchel I was very pleased to see you as well," "Come and meet Grandad", "Hello my dear". He got up and put his arms round me, "I'm very pleased to meet you".
There was photographs everywhere, I was staggered to think how they manage to bring up nine children in that house. "I really hope we will be seeing a lot more of you in the future", she put her arms round both of us and said goodbye. I could see she thought a lot of Ted, and he of her.
We went back to Ted's house, "I've got the kettle boiling, would you like a cup of coffee before you go?" "That would be lovely". "Barbara, I hope we'll see a lot more of you in the future and I don't only mean in the shop". "Mrs Rogers I've had a wonderful afternoon".

Kath and his Mum and Dad waved goodbye, and Ted and me were on our way home.

We said our usual goodbyes, I said "see you Wednesday, Love you".

Dad was a pick-and-shovel man in a gang working for a firm that was putting in mains water and mains sewage pipes.

One day the milk man delivering to one of the houses close by, came running out shouting to Dad, "Walt, I'm sure those two lads are messing about with a bomb", he had no sooner said it when there was an almighty bang, the shed fell apart.

Dad, with one other man, ran out the trench and up the garden path, they were the two lads that belonged to our boxing club, one was killed outright, the two men tried to help the other one but he died on the way to hospital.

It was that night that he decided to finish with the club, Mum and I sat down with him and talked, and he said how that bang and jumping out the trench brought back memories of war. Everyone knew there was only one place where they could have found the bomb, and that was Kingsley Vale, a big natural valley in the South Downs, a lovely place to walk until the military took it over and used it as a bombing range and blew the place apart. After the war it was used for filming some parts of the film "Battle of Britain" and then taken over by the National Trust.

This upset him very much, Mum gave him a cuddle and calmed him down, then I left them alone for a while.

Well, I'm going to hand up my gloves also, you know Barbara and me are very friendly and want to see more of each other. I played one more Game of football and finished the following week.

On her half days off Barbara would go with her friends and sister for cycle rides, one day between them they decided to come through West Stoke to see if they could see me in one of the fields, but I was nowhere to be seen so they carried on, got to the hill going down, not knowing which way to go, some went one way some went the other, the rest went straight up the vicarage Drive and somehow they all ended up together.

The vicar hearing the commotion he rounded them all up took them inside, his wife mended a few cut and scratches. After a chat, he looked up at Barbara, "I think I know this young lady, I have seen you walking up the village once or twice with Ted Rogers", "Yes you have" "Where have you all come from?" "Lavant", was the answer.

Thanking the Vicar and his wife they eventually all got on their bikes and made their way home. On Wednesday he told Barbara he'd finished with boxing and football.

Although they had visited one another's houses, and walked up the old chalk pit lane and over the downs, because they had taken on another assistant in the shop that gave Barbara more time off

Granny, one day talking to Ted, "You're very fond of Barbara aren't you, are we going to hear good news soon?"

Ted had already made up his mind what he was going to do, sometime before they had casually looked in the jeweller's window, jokingly she picked out a ring she would like, and no more was said.

He had already had his eighteenth birthday in September, in the following January 15th on her 18th birthday walking in the snow back to her home over the downs we stopped and I took a box from my pocket, took it out, "That's the one I liked".

"Well, will you marry me?" She cried and laughed, "Of

course I will, what will Mum say?" "We'd better get down the hill and find out". We got to the house both on tenterhooks, went in, they had had their dinner and were sitting down quietly, "Oh I didn't keep any dinner for you" "It's alright Mum, we had a bit at Ted's".

"We've got something to tell you", she held out her hand, "What's this?" She jumped out the chair, flung her arms round both of us and gave us a kiss. "George what do you think of that?"
"Well, there's only one thing and that's a drink", he went to the cupboard came out with a bottle of sherry.
"Have you decided when?" "Well, now Teds given up his boxing and football that will give us more time together. We did think we might wait a year" "Oh that's wonderful, a Christmas wedding, George".
George came up with a surprise, "Barbara would you like to learn to Drive? That will be another wedding present" She was cock-a-hoop, and well, it will be handy one day I am sure of that. "Leave it to me I will make all the arrangements".

"Have you told your Mum and Dad yet?" "No but I know they will be very pleased".
"Have you walked over the downs, and you've got to walk all the way back" "Yes but I'll go round the road". "Tell your Mum I'll see her in the shop on Thursday".
We said our goodbyes and I was well, on my way when a car pulled up, the window wound down" "Hello Ted, I thought it was you". Of all the people, it was my Boss, "what are you doing out this way". I told him, I'd just taken my girlfriend home, and who she was, "Not George Smith's daughter. Well, now, that's a coincidence, I was at the farm talking to him the other day, that's where I've just come from, I had a meeting with his Boss".

"Well, there may be some changes at home on the farm, you know my son Robert, he's finished at the farm where he's been working for some time, now he's coming back home to help me run the farm and be a partner".
"Well, does this mean I'm going to have to find you a house, Ted?" "Oh it won't be for some time yet" "Well, you know Bill and Stan will be retiring later this year, and the council have nearly finished building those six new council bungalows. That was the agreement I had with the council when they wanted that bit of ground, so that will be two houses empty, I can see a few changes coming Ted, I'll drop you off here, I shall see you in the morning".
I had a quick look round the rabbit boxes to make sure they had food and water. Mum saw through the window, "Are you coming in, I'm making a drink?"
"Mum I've got something to tell you, are you ready for a surprise?" "Well, it depends if it's a nice one or not". "I've asked Barbara if she will marry me" "Oh you haven't", "I gave her a ring, she said' yes she would so we were engaged".
"Does her Mum know?" "We told her parents this afternoon, she was over the moon", "Of course we all will be, and Granny will be cock-a-hoop". "Well, her Mum said she would like to meet up with you on Thursday at the shop about 2 o'clock".

The garage at Lavant realised that there was a need for a bus service around the villages and it was very welcome for the women to go shopping, they both arrived within minutes of each other at the shop, Barbara was quickly with them and introduced them to one another. Barbara had already mentioned to Beryl of the meeting, they both shook hands and both agreed it was wonderful news. Her Mum jumped in first, "I'm Elsie", "and I'm Edith, I can't believe we have been doing our shopping here all these years and not known one another, they have kept it a secret for long time".

Elsie said "What time will your bus go?" "I've got about two hours" "Yours is a bit earlier than mine, can I suggest we hand Mrs Dobbs our list and we go over the road to the coffee shop and have a coffee and a chat and pick our groceries up later?"

Barbara, had gone back behind the counter, but Beryl had heard all the excitement and with a smile said "Barbara would you like to go with them for half an hour? I can see it's a special occasion".

"Well, Elsie, it looks like we've got a Christmas wedding on our hands, all we've got to do is let those two choose a date".

"Mum, I must get back. It's been lovely getting you together I'm sure you will have plenty to talk about".

Elsie said "I know the first thing I have got to do is book the village hall or it will be too late, so the weekend if you agree. Pick out some Saturday date around Christmas and we will let them choose".

The two Mums finished their coffee and walked back to the shop to collect their groceries, "We have picked some dates around Christmas, you pick which one. We had a wonderful chat, now we've got to go and catch our buses, I will see you later, be careful coming home" "It's alright Mum Eileen will be with me".

On the way, I told her Ted had asked me to marry him, "You're pulling my leg" "Come round the weekend".

This was put to Ted and Barbara, "I'll agree whatever you want" "Well, I think December 20th will be nice, that's the date your Mum picked".

Just then Eileen came knocking, "Come in" Mum called to her, just in time for the news "George, give Eileen a glass" "I know what you're going to tell me, I can't believe it". "Well, you better, because that's the date Elsie said, 20th December".

Sister Sheila grabbed Eileen, Barbara and Elsey and danced around, "it looks as if they have made their mind up, Ted".

The Boss has already told me there will be two houses coming empty when the chaps retire later this year. I'd know which one I'd got my eye on, I know Barbara will like it, when we have been out walking up the village she often commented on it, there was a big garden and at the end a very nice piece of ground which was, an old allotment and was waste and scrub land, I knew it belonged to the Boss.

There was never a day went by on my way to work, I turned it over in my mind what I could do with that piece of ground. One day out walking with Barbara, I let her see what I had in mind, "Pigs", she said "but look at the mess it's in" "Well, pigs will clean it up after a while". "I kept this to myself until now and that's the house we will have, the Boss already promised me that. I haven't mentioned the piece of ground yet, I will the first chance I get".

"Bill will be moving out in September, what do you think of that idea? I know between us we could make it work"

"Well, I helped Dad with the cattle so I am sure I could handle pigs".

"I would like to keep this to ourselves until I have sorted it with the Boss".

"I promise" and sealed it with a kiss.

Chapter 3

Ted and Barbara got married

My Mum and Elsie had met a number of time in the town discussing who was going to do what and when.
The harvest had just about finished, and every year the Boss would put on a small harvest supper for the workers and all those who had helped through the year. It was always held in the village hall, Bill always made it quite a knees-up playing his accordion and singing.
I made sure Barbara's Mum and Dad were invited, half way through the evening the Boss banged on the table and a glass in his hand, "I'd like you all to join me in wishing Ted and Barbara best wishes on their forthcoming wedding on December 20th". That was very unexpected. Suddenly the room went quiet who should walk in but the village Vicar, the Boss shouted, "Come in Vicar grab a glass and join the party I'm glad you could make it, and Mrs Lines" he was quickly told the news and wished us both good wishes, he quietly said "I look forward to reading your bands in church in December I expect the Lavant vicar will have the pleasure of your wedding".
The evening was gradually coming to a close, goodbyes and hugs all round, my Mum and Dad made their way home just down the road, a mate of mine took George and Elsie and Barbara and dropped them off on his way home. The next day Sunday I rode over to Barbara's house, Elsie and George were over the moon about the party, Elsie said "You know you will have to see the vicar to book the church and to call your bands". "Well, there's no time like the present, why don't we cycle down to the church tonight shall we Ted? It don't start until 6 o'clock, we will have plenty of time", "okay let's do that".

We arrived at the church, this took me back to my school

days, the vicar's name was Dunlop, the school was right next door, the vicarage was just across the road, I remember it was well guarded by a pair of geese.

Although it was officially Barbara's church, she used to go to the little one at the other end of the village. We were about the last to arrive, he stood at the door shaking hands with everyone, "Barbara, how nice to see you and where have you found this young man? Goodness let me think". He seemed to have forgotten he had a church full of people waiting for him, "I remember Ted Rogers, the boy we could always rely on to win a football match or cricket match for us".

Barbara gave me a nudge, "Oh vicar, do you think we could have a chat after the service?" "Yes of course you may wait for me inside". He practically ran in and we quickly found us a seat.

The service over, he took us to the vestry, "Now, when I get a young couple come to see me, I only get one thought in my mind, I'm right, you would like to get married?" "Yes, you are right". "Can you tell me the whole story? Barbara, you went to West Dean School, but you did go to my Little Church and your church

Ted was at West Stoke, but I am sure that I have seen you both at our youth club, and you've been together all these years, Well, I think it's wonderful".

"Have you thought of a date yet?", "We would like it to be December the 20th"" "Oh a Christmas wedding". Barbara quickly said "I would very much like this church". "Well, I have the diary here let's see, would you like me to give you a time, how about 3 o'clock December 20th"" We both thanked him, "Your bands will be called 3 weeks before-hand every week, but I hope we will see you many times before then". I knew I was going to catch the Boss and will have to put the idea to him. He told me some time ago that he could see big changes coming in the village, also to the farm. My chance came one morning, he called us into the office one at a time, it was a bit of a shock. "Now Bill and Stan has retired, they won't be replaced, and I'm sorry too that four of the horses will be going and replaced by Fordson tractors, and this is where you come in Ted, I want you and Jim to Drive them. This means that the future of farming is going to change very quickly all over the country".

"I promised you the house Ted and that still stands, so if you and Barbara want to go and do any decorating to your liking, just get the key from the office". "Boss can I have a word with you about something else"? "What's that Ted", "Well, you know the old allotments adjoining the garden which is in a bit of a mess? I know it belongs to the farm, I wondered if you would consider renting it to me. If I clear it, my idea would be to keep a pig or two on it, fenced in properly".

"Robert, have you ever thought about that bit of ground", he said to his son, "Well, it would look better if it was tidied up a bit Dad". "Here's what I'll do Ted, being as I know you so well, as a wedding present you have it for a year free and thereafter we have another agreement like the house, it's a tied cottage notice, I'll get the secretary to draw up an agreement".

It was late that night when I left work, I called in and told Mum what I'd done, "I thought you had that in mind, Barbara will be over the moon when you tell her", "I'm going over there now", "I'll keep your tea for you, try not to be late".

I was on my old bike and I peddled like never before, I got to their house earlier than thought. Elsie spotted me coming down the road, "Barbara, I thought you said Ted won't be over tonight". They met me by the door there was always a peck on the cheek from Elsie and a better one from Barbara.

"I hope I've got some good news for you" Sheila said "You've always got good news Ted", "Well, I had a word with the Boss today, he said we can go in the house and do any decorating we want, but we've got time before that". Barbara looked at me "And what else" She knew I had something else on my mind, "Well, he said I can have the old allotment ground free for a year as a wedding present and to keep pigs on it if I want and talk about it again after a year, and Robert agreed with all this.

"This is going to mean I will have to do more over-time and piece-work, I've already bought some posts and wire netting, so if you don't see me for a bit, you know where I am, and I will come and find you".

George had been in his shed all this time and just came to hear most of it, "I wondered what all the excitement was all about, wonderful news".

Next day at work we were told that the rest of the horses were going and two more tractors were coming, it was going to be a complete turnaround, but between us all we seem to get the work done.

Our families were getting on sorting out wedding arrangements, my sister Kathleen and Barbara's sister Sheila were to be bride's maids and surprise for Eileen she was asked to be maid of honour, she was absolutely thrilled to bits, and my brother Bob was best man.

My Mum had already made two cakes, the shop promised Barbara some discount on the food, and Granny of course had to be involved. Mum shouted at me one day, "You haven't got your suit yet, you're coming with me this afternoon and don't forget".

Invitations had been sent out, my brother Wally had seen to the cars that were needed and was pleased he was going to Drive Barbara and her Dad to church. We had decided we were not going to have a honeymoon, the house we were having was ready for us to move into.

The wedding went to plan, the party after was very good, my Boss and George's Boss thanked us for inviting them. The field I was having was about ready, so after Christmas I went to see Tom Mortimer, who I had spoken to before about buying a gilt or two, the one I want Tom, to start with is one that's in pig. "Well, there's a bunch Ted, pick one of these gilts Landrace cross Large white", "What do you want for this one Tom?" I had a chalk marker with me, "She's well in pig, I want seventy pounds for that" "I tell you what, Tom, I'll give you seventy pound if you will deliver it to where I want her", we shook hands and we agreed.

I made sure Barbara knew what to do when she came, I allowed her about a quarter of the pen, and Tom brought her the next day

Barbara was up at the pen when Tom came, "Good morning Mrs Rogers", "And to you Mr Mortimer", she opened the gate, Tom dropped the tailboard of the trailer. The pig after a bit of coaxing walked out into the pen, Tom closed the trailer door, "There you are my dear, she's all yours, tell Ted to give me a shout if there is any problems".

We had noticed there was a lot of activity going on across the fields, but no one took much notice.

Barbara and I still walked across the downs, but not so much now we had our own home, the local vicar on his usual walk round was breaking the news of his retirement and the clergy was not replacing him, the vicarage was up for sale.

Not long after that we were all invited up to the main hall for a late village Christmas party. This year it was quite late on. The squire welcomed everybody with his usual speech, but this year with a sad tone to it. With his wife by his side, he announced that he was selling the estate and retiring to live in the vicarage which they had bought.

I was standing on the big lawn with my brother Wally and his wife, he wanted to work there when he came out of the merchant navy. It suddenly hit me that it was one of the big changes that my Boss had told me a long time ago was coming.

This put a stop to the hurdle making and spars for thatching locally and the chestnut and hazel coppicing. It wasn't long before my brother had found another job on an estate in Hampshire following on in forestry as before.

My pig now had her young and to our delight she had ten healthy piglets, and I bought another young gilt.

The estate was bought by people who only wanted to make a huge profit, there was no communicating with the village as it was soon evident the woodlands soon became bare, the huge parkland had been cleared for machinery to work the land and rolled and mowed it just to produce turf. But we really thought the Home Farm was alright, the Boss told us that Patha News was coming to film the farm, we had a new combine harvester delivered and thing were looking good.

Two weeks later Robert told us, the Boss had told him to take us all in to Chichester to see the film and a meal after.

Our second pig farrowed, but she only had six young ones, the first litter was coming up to ten weeks ready for weaning and then to market. Barbara helped me get them ready, the trick was split them in two pens, bit of straw and give them a good rub with talcum powder, this made them look really good.

Tom was there as usual, always ready for a good deal he came and stood beside, this was the first time Barbara had been to an auction she held my hand.

Each pen was sold separately 20pounds start me 25, 30, 40, all done and sold. A tear came in her eyes, the second pen same again he shouted 30 pounds 35, 40 pounds all done and sold,80 pounds she whispered, Tom looked across put his thumb up in approval.

We just managed and caught the bus home, for the next few days in the village was talk about the farm film stars and of course the activity going on across the fields, it was gravel they were looking for.

Then one morning no Boss or Robert came out, but we all knew what our jobs were, so we just went ahead and dun them. Dinner time came Robert was waiting in the yard, he called us all together, "I'm afraid I've got some bad news for you all, he held his breath for a bit. Father past away last night in his sleep".

What a shock for everybody, "But I know he would want you to carry on with me the same as you did with him".

I often wondered about the old horse drawn wagon that was kept in the garden unbeknown to us. Two of our old shire horses had been put into a retirement home and cleaned up for the purpose and the wagon.

Bill and Stan were called on from retirement to lead the pair with the coffin to the church, we all knew how much he loved the shires.

George had decided he had enough of farm work, they bought a café, Sheila married a Yorkshire farmer, after a while they sold the café and moved up Yorkshire and between them bought a hotel.

I came home one day, Barbara was rather quiet, I asked what was wrong, "I'm going to have a baby", I was over the moon, and she said "I walked down the road this afternoon and had a chat with your Mum, she was very pleased, well, we all are. But this will upset all your plans now" "Don't worry we will sit down and sort things out I promise", it was obvious with a baby on the way I could not spend any more on the pigs, so I just kept the first gilt on and the second one with her litter of seven, and sell them as porkers later on.

There was a bit of unrest in the village with the vicar leaving and the squire selling the estate to newcomers who did not want to fit in with village life, and the activity across the fields getting closer. But the farm still carried on, Barbara had given up her job at the shop so that made our income less but we still managed.

My Mum went up the village to see if Barbara was alright but realised what was going on and called the midwife. I came home at dinner time and sat with her for dinner.

Mum said "You can go back to work if you've got to, I'll stay with her, the midwife is coming back this afternoon" I could not wait till 5 o'clock, but I had to finish what I was doing so it was gone 5 when I got home.

I was told to have a wash and go up and see Barbara, I opened the door and there sat up in bed with a baby in her arms, "It's a boy". A big kiss and a big cuddle was needed, Mum stayed until I had fed our pigs, she said her goodbyes, "I'll come up first thing in the morning so you can go back to work, the nurse will come later", that was December 5th just in time for Christmas.

The baby was christened a few weeks later Trevor Frances.

"A note was in my pay packet, "Ted, will you come and see me before you go home, Mrs Pam Mason who was the Bosses' wife, Robert's mother wants to see you". I went straight to the back door and the maid took me in, "Ted, congratulations on your baby boy, come into the lounge". "Now about the piece of land you've cleared. It seems to me that it was never going to come back to be worked by the farm, so I have instructed Robert for as long as you work for him, no one pays house rent and continue to have the old allotments free. I want you to keep this letter signed by Robert and myself".
"I'm sad to say I will be moving out from the farm, Robert will be moving in with his wife and family very soon. I wish you and Barbara great happiness and good luck in the future".
I shook her hand firmly and wished her a happy retirement I said goodbye, the maid Margaret showed me out and whispered, "I'm going with her".
On my way home I looked in on the pigs, with the piece of paper in my hand, I felt sure this was something to do with him. (The Boss)
I was dreaming of what I could do, a little voice came from behind me, "I wondered where you got to, and it's alright Mum got the baby, and I have fed the pigs for you". I showed her the piece of paper, "That's marvellous this means we won't have to find rent", she grabbed my arm and said "Come on let's get some tea". Mum had a good old stew going, "I'll take a bit of this stew back for Dad he always likes stew, Ted you know I'm only down the road if you want me, I will see you in the morning".
I suppose with my brothers moving away and my sister with living her boyfriend, we kind of filled the gap. The farm got more mechanised anyone retiring was never replaced, the local casual workers wasn't needed now electricity and mains water and sewage was all working.

All the village wells were sealed over for safety.
How right the Boss was all those years ago when he gave me a lift home and told me he could see big changes coming to the village. The cattle herd was growing, machine milking took over from hand milking, which meant less men needed, they didn't like the idea of over-time or piece-work.
I rather liked it, it was the right work for me, it fitted in with our pigs and my Dad was beginning to slow down a bit now and was showing an interest in our pigs. He wanted to help a bit more because the pick and shovel job wasn't needed that was mechanically done, so with the chickens and rabbits and a bit we give them on the side he got by all right.

Another baby was on the way, three years had gone by and this one was due in August, another Christmas came and went by.
Our baby was running around now, Barbara had started to help Dad with the chickens and rabbits, my Mum helped out a lot by looking after Trevor. The time simply flew by, I bought two more gilts so between us we were pretty busy, that was as many sows I could keep on that bit of ground. I kept well in touch with Tom, he always knew when to bring one of his boars to work, he also kept his eye on the litter and was always ready to buy on the field which saved me the journey to market.
 The work across the fields was getting closer, this resulted in Lorries coming through the village and questions were being asked.
Robert came out one morning and was very upset, you've all got a month to stay on for the new owners or find other work, the farm has been sold completely out of my control, I'll speak to each of you separately and explain. My turn came, he said he was very sorry, but that was not

good enough for me, I was hedge trimming that day and trying to earn a bit of extra, so I quizzed him to tell me more.

"Well, you can see how close the gravel people are pushing one side of the estate on the other, the offer I got to sell was ridiculous. The advice I got from my mother and Uncle was well approved, I can tell you, Ted, the buyers are Heever Brothers as you know they are massive contracting firm".

That night to my surprise Tom came knocking, Barbara answered the door, "Mr Mortimer come in", "Is Ted in?" she would not have asked him in if he was not, "I hope I'm not intruding", "No of course not, what can I do for you?" "Well, it's more what I can do for you. I'll come straight to the point, I heard the bad news this afternoon, if it's going to help, Ted, I know the pigs' breeding, and I know how well, they have been looked after. I'll buy them off you, and all your wire and posts and put cash on the table now".

I heard that he was a bit of a wheeler dealer but he was always fair with me. Barbara butted in, "Mr Mortimer would you like a cup of tea?" "Oh yes please", on her way out she gave me a slight glance and winked. Her eye this I took to be, don't be so eager, she came back in with the tea and a plate of Mums homemade cakes, I was still mulling it over in my mind, I thought five hundred pounds. He helped himself to another piece of cake, "Now Ted" pulling out a wad of notes, "how about five hundred and fifty, well, there's several bags of food".

"Right, If I take the pigs tomorrow, you take and roll up the wire and posts down for me", he pulled another two hundred and fifty pounds, put it with the other, "have we got a deal". I looked at Barbara, she nodded in approval, we shook hands.

"Now one other thing, you will be looking for another job,

you've heard of Lady McDougall, yes, she got a farm a bit further along the Downs, well I was talking to her farm manager Mr Lownds, the other day he asked me if I came across a good lad to send him his way, I got his phone number with me, it's not too late to go and give him a ring now, ring him from the box up the road. I'll ring him also when I get home let me know tomorrow how you got on".
I got through to him and apologised for ringing a bit late, I told him who I was, he said "Are you Walt's son?" I said "Yes I am" I told him.
"Tom Mortimer told me you might be looking for a farm hand" "Well, I know we have met before a few times, I will have a word with her ladyship. Tomorrow is Friday our shopping day, come and see me the next day Saturday morning at ten o'clock at the farm office, we will have a chat then.
I got back home Barbara was a bit upset, a kiss and a cuddle calmed her down, "Did you really expect as much as that?" Well, I know he's a crafty old boy, he won't be the loser, but I promise you I will never be out of work.
You know that I have told you that Lady McDougall the flower people who live at the other end of the downs, but I'm sorry to say that's the end of my dream, I'm going for an interview on Saturday morning. I think it's time we went to bed, the children have been asleep all evening".

Saturday morning came, I'd already been out and rolled up some wire, I got ready to go, Barbara wished me luck, "I won't take any house until you have seen the house".
I arrived on time, Mr Lownds welcomed me into the office, it's a bad job about Masons farm, Robert was being squeeze on both sides, and it's a shame to see the village being spoilt. But I'm glad to say that will never happen here, one thing we've got no gravel it's all chalk, as you probably see as you came in we have a pretty big flock of

sheep and beef cattle, I understand you can turn your hand to anything. "Well, I like hedge laying and most kinds of fencing, at the moment there's four of us at the moment with myself, but her ladyship tells me to take things a bit easier and give the men a bit more overtime", "Well, that suits me".

"Well, Ted, I think I know enough about you, but if you would like to come over this afternoon with your wife, I was going to ask about that, I would like her to see the house. Well, if she's happy with the house I would like to offer you the job which will be the agricultural wage and two substantial bonuses with plenty of over time. We will lay on a removal van, so if you hand in your notice and we will move you in two weeks' time. In the meantime I will make an appointment for you and your wife to meet her ladyship, I will pop down and see you one evening. A mate of mine gave me a lift up to the big house".

At the time when the tractors were coming to the farm, I was one of the men to take a test I also knew the person who gave driving lessons, he told me to book a test for a car, he would see that I had his car. I passed the tractor test first time which took place on the farm. I had to take the car test twice which was in town.

I never told much of this to Barbara because I knew then there was no chance of having a car. But now having got rid of the pigs, and some spare money I talked it over with her, I was sorry I did not tell her at the time, she was glad I did not tell her with everything else going on at the time, but perhaps we can think a bit more about it now.

The manager met us at the bottom of the Drive, my mate said he would come later to pick us up, Mr Lownds thanked him and offered to take us home himself. "Just one thing Ted, she likes to be called madam or mam, the maid came to the door, "Hullo Mr Lownds, Madam will see you in the dining room, come in", she obviously knew him as Richard, "Good evening madam, I'd like to introduce you to Ted and Barbara Rogers who I have already spoke to you about".

Yes I understand you're pretty good at hedge laying, I have always wanted our hedges laid, we have a few acres of hazel and chestnut, would that be any good?" "It certainly would, I can make sheep hurdles and if you wanted it coppiced, the chestnut would make good fencing stakes".

"Well, Barbara, its all about the job at the moment, you have two children, have you seen the house".

It was about fifty yards from the one next to it, which was a barn conversion and was occupied by another farm worker. The one we're going in three bedrooms, kitchen /dining room and a very big lounge which looked across the Downs. A very big adjoining out house which had drying facilities and another storage compartments, a big garden for the children to play in, Trevor was about to start school and there was a school taxi to pick him up and bring him home, which Barbara was pleased with..

"Yes, it looks quite new, it was built six years ago it will go with your job, it has got all mod con's, it has not been occupied as much as we were hoping, but I can say someone has gone in once a week to keep it well aired and clean".

"Richard, can I leave things with you to see they settle in? I quite look forward to having the woodlands sorted, and of course making our own sheep hurdles.

Once you are settled in I will come and see you. Richard, I meant to ask you if you told Barbara, you run the mini bus every Friday to take the ladies shopping, I forgot the children". Ted quickly said "That won't be a problem, my mother will fill that gap".

But what I did not know was, the old Boss's maid's sister, Betty Combs was married to the other farm worker, Tom Combs, who had a car and kindly offered to pick my Mum up to sit with the children while they all went shopping in the mini bus Friday mornings.

The Sunday morning we walked down the road to have a coffee with Mum and Dad and explain everything to them, Dad did say he had got rid of a lot of the chickens and rabbits, sold all the ferrets to a local lad who always said he would like them .

I told them once we had settled in, I would buy a car and come and see them and they will always be welcome to come and have a holiday with us, and that goes for my next brother who was still working on the estate, but did not know how much longer he could put up with it.

We went back home for dinner, it seemed very strange not having something to do, suddenly I said, you know what I'd like to do, how about walking up the old chalk pit lane and over the Downs we'll take the children they have never been that far, I knew we would have to carry them part of the way. It wasn't until we got nearly to the top of the lane that I realised how serious things were getting.

When I think how I used to dig out lumps of chalk and cut up into blocks, and now it's just being used as a big dumping hole.

We walk up to the top of the hill right to the spot where I asked Barbara to marry me. Trevor said, "What have we stopped for Dad" We look down across the other side to where Barbara's home used to be, Well, I don't think any of us will ever stand here again, we held hand and slowly walked back down.

It wasn't too hot but we had taken a drink with us there was a number of sheep roaming around us, Barbara gave a little giggle, "Daddy will be working with sheep now and not pigs", Pauline said in her own way, "Pig all gone". Barbara said "I thought her ladyship was very nice", "Yes she seemed to be a bit excited about having the woodlands sorted, I just wonder how bad they are and also the hedges".

"Well, we will know in two weeks' time, there's one thing you've got all your axes and hooks, shall we go home and have tea? I bet you both will sleep tonight with all that lovely fresh air".

We never called on Mum and Dad we thought we'd let them have a quiet afternoon. Barbara had given then a key if ever they wanted to get in. The door was ajar the children could not wait to get in, ran straight into Granny's arms they had to tell her where they had been. Up on the Downs, to see the sheep and big Lorries and tractors.

Look, I've got some drink ready for you and tea will be ready for you when you want it, we've got enough for all of us. The talk was all about the job, and the house, I think you will like it.

Dad said "you'll be giving in your notice tomorrow morning", "yes I will". He said "I don't think there will be many village lads stopping on the estate or farm, Brother Wally is going for a job close to Andover in Hampshire, it a job he's been looking for a long time, head forester on a very big estate".

"I didn't tell you, him and Peggy, and the two girls will be calling round later tonight, I was coming down to get you later but you beat us to it, you know I told you, they lay a mini bus on a Friday mornings if you and Mum still want to come to us, then I got someone to come and fetch you if we give her something for the petrol which of course we will. We had tea and settled down when they turned up and of course it was all talk about our jobs.

Wally said if all this upheaval had come later there probably will be a job on the estate where we are going, well we are moving in a fortnight's time. Barbara came up with the idea, can we promise where ever we go we keep in touch with each other, we know Mum and Dad has never had a holiday, can we agree from time to time we have them come and stay with each of us for a while.

Mum broke down and cried and gave Barbara and Peggy a big kiss and a cuddle.

"Now, Trevor and Pauline, it's time for bed, give everyone a goodnight kiss" and off to bed they went. Barbara came down they hardly touched the pillow and they were asleep, Barbara said "I'll make us all a drink".

Wally had bought a car some time ago, Peggy asked "are you going to get one?" "Ted's got his eye on one when we've moved, here's our new address and when you go, write to us to let us know how you are going on". "Well, you never know, I might take a quick driving test" Realising she had learnt to Drive before we had married and taken her test and passed, but we were never able to afford a car. Barbara said "I really must write a letter to Mum and Dad tomorrow and give them all the news and our new address and start packing a few things. It doesn't seem long since we moved in here".

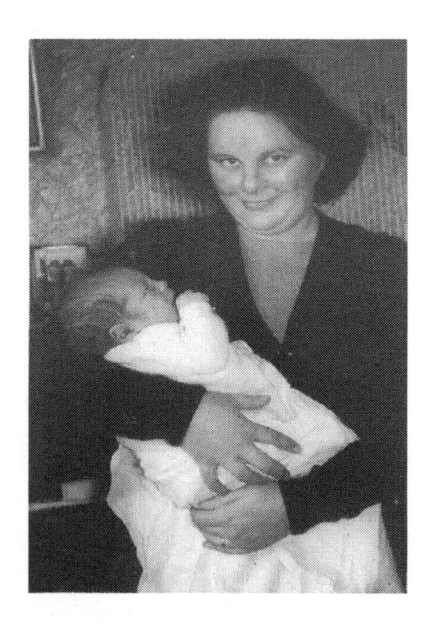

Barbara with first born child Trevor see page 40

Chapter 4

Our First Car

I handed in my notice to Jane the secretary next morning, she told me how she was told she would not be wanted any longer, she could not believe how the village was being pulled apart. I was surprised how much money I had to come on the last pay day when I made out my time sheet, piece work and overtime came to quite a bit, so three of us went to the office to get it verified and came away very pleased. I also had a day's holiday owing so I finished work on Thursday. I came home deep in thought, Barbara could see I had something on my mind, she asked what I was thinking about.

"Well, what would you say if I said I'd a good mind to cycle over to Lavant Garage and see if they've still got the car for sale which I've had my eye on, well, it's your money in the bank as well as mine and you know I always keep some cash by us.
It won't be a very big car or a posh car, but it will do us for a while, and we will still have some money by us from the pigs we sold, I know we will have a lift in for shopping Fridays but we won't be anywhere near the bus service which neither of us thought about until now so it might make sense to have a car to be independent.
If I go now I'll get over there before they close, as luck would have it the chap on duty was a lad I knew Tony Bleech, I played football with him so we had a good chat. I got round to asking him if the car was still for sale, the Ford Popular, do you want a chat with the Boss Mr Bleech, "Hello, Ted it's been a long time since we last met, what's going on at West Stoke? I hear they're tearing the village apart".

Well, that's one reason I'm leaving here on Saturday, that's why I came over here tonight to look at this car and do a deal with you now, "Well, it belongs to an old lady in the village and we have maintained it for a number of years so it's in good condition, she has got too old to Drive it now so she wants rid of it. It's got Tax and Insurance for six months and it's got three months to run, what sort of price are you willing to pay for it Ted?".
"Well, can I have a look at it first" "Of course you can, Tony fetch it out and go with Ted let him have a Drive in it". I was quite surprise how good it looked and how good I felt driving it.
We got back and I remember some of Tom Mortimer's words "Hesitate and Ponder" right Mr Bleech I know how much I can go up to, you tell me how much you want for it. "Well, the old lady said she would be happy with around eight hundred pounds", what sort of guarantee can you give me for that, "it won't be a very big one he smiled". I walked around the car, I did like it and I thought how pleased Barbara would be if I went back and said I could pick it up tomorrow morning.
"I tell you what I can do, if you give me six months guarantee have it ready for me to pick up in the morning about eleven o'clock and all the paper work that goes with it, I'll give you eight hundred and fifty pounds". He said "You make it nine hundred tomorrow morning and it's yours with everything you want", we shook hands, "Thank you Ted, I can promise you it's a nice little car".
I called in on the way home and told Mum and Dad what I'd done, and will pick you both up Saturday morning early, and we can look after the children while you're busy and you can come with us to see the house". I quickly said goodbye, see you Saturday morning and jumped on the old bike thinking thank goodness I won't be riding this

think much more.

I was a bit late getting back the children had gone to bed, we had a nice cup of tea. "Well, come on, tell me the bad news". I said "it's a Ford Popular, black and got four wheels" "Oh don't be horrible" "No darling I'm only teasing, but it is a Ford Popular and black and I hope you will be pleased, I paid nine hundred pounds and it's taxed and insured for six months and fully guaranteed for six month and I can pick it up in the morning".

She gave me a big hug, "Now we've got to sort out some money before we go to bed".

"Well, that's no problem, he'll take five hundred cash and four hundred cheque, is that all right?" "Yes I'm happy with that" she agreed.

We went to bed thinking about how things had changed since we got married. I woke early next morning took a walk up the garden looked at the field where the pigs were and across the farm where the horses used to be, I could hear some noise of machinery in the distance, I did not want to hear that. Went back to the house Barbara was still in bed, I took a cup of tea up to her she was just like her Mum for a cup of tea, she was beginning to wake up. "Is it time we were up?" "There's no hurry yet". She looked at me, have I been dreaming or have we really bought a car, yes we have bought a car and I am going to get it this morning.

"I think I'll walk over because I won't be able to bring back the bike, it will only take me an hour or so. You get the children up and I'll go down and do the breakfast, then it will be time for me to go".

I was on my way and passed a short distance from all the quarry activity, I quickly went past it and tried to put it out of my mind, I got to the garage Mr Bleech was tinkering with other cars, Tony was in the office and gave his Dad a shout, we said good morning to each other and went into the office. "I've got all the paper work, Ted" I hope it won't be a problem Mr Bleech, will you accept five hundred in cash and a four hundred in cheque, "that's what we agreed Ted", I handed the money over and he gave me the paper work and a written guarantee, we shook hands and went out to the car. "There she is Ted, I hope you and your family will have many happy miles travelling and don't be afraid to give me a call if you have any trouble with it, you have got half a tank of petrol so that will get you around a bit".

On my way home all sorts of things going round in my head, before I knew it I had pulled up outside the house, she must have seen me pull up as she was stood waiting at the gate with Trevor and Pauline, I don't think I have seen her with such a big smile on her face for a long time. Before I could say anything the children were sat in the back, Barbara in the driving seat, "I'm going to Drive this" she said, "I could not agree with you more you Drive it".

"Let's have some dinner, you know we could go for a Drive this afternoon, would you like that, shall we give Mum and Dad a surprise?" "You mean take them out" "Well, if they're looking after the children for us sometimes" Barbara said "You go down and tell them to be ready".

"I'll get our dinner and we will pick them up after" Well, it did not take long to get over dinner, we were in the car and down the road, I went in and got them, "What's this?" "Would you like to come for a ride" They got in the back, Trevor was small enough to sit in the middle, and Pauline on Nan's lap. "I cannot believe this", she kept saying the further we went Grandad said, "Oh I know where we are going, it's a while since I've been round here, we eventually got to a spot where we could see the big house, Grandad said "That's where Lady McDougall lives up that long Drive". Ted said, "That's where she lives, now I can show you where we are going to live tomorrow" We went on a bit further to the next Driveway, this is why we had to have a car, we stopped at the first house, I've got the key so we can go in". Mum, while we are here Ted and I will nip down to the next house and let Betty and Tom know what's going on, we saw them in the garden and we shook hands and explained we did not get the car until this morning".

Betty said "I'm glad you're moving in tomorrow we must get together and have a good old chat, with my two, Jane and Susan and yours and of course Ted. You knew my sister Jane she is having to leave. I'll pop down tomorrow when you come, to see if there's anything you need" "Thanks Betty, we must go Teds Mum and Dad are at the house having a look round with the children".

We got back and Nan said "What a beautiful view you got across the downs" Grandad said "I bet there's a good many rabbit up there Ted" "Yes and I believe there is a problem with foxes with the lambs, a lot of them got to be got rid of".

Ted asked "Have you all had a good look round? Have you seen all those sheep out there? It looks like they will soon want shearing. I wonder what my first job will be. Well, I got a surprise for someone" Nan said "Well, it can't be us because we have had a wonderful time haven't we Grandad? "Well, I did not expect to come up here today".

"Right, Nan and Grandad in the back with Trevor, Pauline on Nan's lap but this time Mum's going to Drive" "I haven't tried yet" she said, "Well, you can take it down the Drive to the road. Just sit in for a minute and think what you did before with your feet on clutch, gears, accelerator, just take it slowly" Well, I did not worry, she took to it no trouble at all, we got to the bottom of the

Drive looked at me and said "I can't believe what I have just done". Nan said "We didn't know you could Drive Barbara" "It's a long time since I have" we swapped over seats and Ted took over.

"Let's go home and have a cup of tea" Nan said, "Take us home first so you can have a quiet evening you will have a busy day tomorrow" He dropped them off as she asked, gave us all a kiss, "We will walk up and see you in the morning".

It was a good job we were up early, eight o'clock, a big posh removal van pulled up, I said to Barbara, "Blimey we get the whole house in that thing". Two men came and asked are you Mr and Mrs Rogers going to Hollings Field Farm, instructions from Lady Mc——, just then, Mr Lownds pulled up, "Good morning, Ted, everything all right?" "Yes thankyou I will pop round to see you later this afternoon".

They got the furniture on and all the boxes and bits and bobs, anything from the garden shed. One of them said, "Lay it alongside the van that can go on last, I did not think I had so much in the shed. We locked up the house, I went to the farm house and dropped the keys through the letter box, the van had just moved off, we were in our little car and followed behind.

Chapter 5

This was the first move (of many to come.)

We arrived at the house just before twelve o'clock, the same man said "Now dear, tell us where and which room you want it in" Nan and Grandad said we will take the children in the garden out the way. It didn't take long to unload. Nan came in, "have you found the kettle yet" Barbara said "yes it's all there in the kitchen" it wasn't long before we all had a cup of tea the men with the van especially.
Grandad and Ted carried the tools and garden stuff into the outhouse and made sure everything was hung up and put into cupboards, when they came in, it did not take long to get most of it sorted out.
Mr Lownds came round later, "Hello, Walt, my word it's a long time since we met, I don't think you met my wife Mrs Rogers". "Now Barbara is everything all right at the moment? If there's anything you're not happy with, let me know. When you get settled, my wife Rosie will pop round.
Ted I see you've got yourself a nice little motor" Yes I did, it was a sudden decision Friday morning we made, at least we will be able to go visiting, we realised the bus service we had before doesn't come anywhere near here".
"Well, that won't make any difference, I will still take you ladies shopping Friday mornings, her ladyship will insist on that. Well, I gather you have met Tom and Betty, and the other lad John you will meet on Monday morning, and you will know me and Richard, they will be getting the pens ready for sheep shearing and you will be in on that later. But first I want you to come with me on Monday, you know her ladyship is keen on the hedges being laid so

that she can see how it looks from the big lawn, well, it's something I like doing. Well, I'll be on my way enjoy the rest of the weekend, goodbye for now".

"Now the first thing we got to do is get you insured, the car is but you're not, but you can Drive it up and down the back Driveway so as to get used to it". Nan asked, "Are you taking us back home? "Yes of course we are after tea if that's all right?" "Well, I think you should have tomorrow on your own, grandad and I have plenty to catch up with".

Trevor and Pauline in the car we are taking nan and grandad back home, Barbara had no hesitation and jumped in the driving seat, I could see she wasn't going to let me do much driving which I was very pleased to see, she drove down the Drive and slowly out onto the road she looked at me and smiled, I nodded in approval outside their house and went in with them.

Ted asked his Dad is there anything he wanted a hand with, no but you can take some of this veg back with you He got a bag and stuffed it full, "That will keep you going for a bit, take some eggs. We've still got half a dozen hens left". Big hugs and kisses, "We will see you in the week, yes we will walk down one evening".

Barbara was in the car raring to go, I must say it was a very quiet road, she pulled into and up the Drive and stopped outside the house, we had quite a hard piece of ground to park on. "I hope your insurance cover will come through, I hope it will cover both of us" I said to Nan "We will walk down one evening" She laughed, and said "more like Drive down all that way".

"Well, it's about time you two went to bed, it's been a very busy day for us all, Pauline's going first, Daddy will you take Trevor?" I got him dried and dressed ready for bed it was very quiet, single beds side by side, he got into his bed, Barbara was flat out fast asleep alongside Pauline reading her a story. I came down stairs and lay on the settee in the lounge looking out across the Downs, before I knew it I was fast asleep, she had woken up, came down and started sorting a few of the coats and shoes and bit and odds and ends, she tried to be quiet, but it was enough to wake me, we really must try to take things easy today, they both agreed.

Sunday was a nice day warm enough to put a blanket on the ground, it's a good job we brought some groceries with us, and who would like an ice cream, and they all shouted we do. Ted was looking across the fields, I can see plenty of hedges, and we can just see the big house from here. That big hedge running right up the Downs, I wonder if that's the one he wants me to tackle first, well, I shall know in the morning.

A voice called out from the road, "Hullo Barbara" it was Tom and Betty from just down the road, come in, would the girls like an ice cream, Jane and Susan yes please. Tom said "I believe you are going to start laying hedges Ted", I am just looking across at that big one at the back of the big house, I'm not surprised if that's the first one on her ladyship's wants sorted, it's a bit of a mess. "The big job next week shearing, Wednesday I think, but he gets two good shearers in, all we do is catch and roll the fleeces and bag it up".

Barbara asked how many are there to shear, "about eight hundred, but there's over a thousand all told, there's another chap Arthur, lives on his own the other side the farm". It's nice to see the girls have got someone to play with, Trevor will soon be going to school. Betty asked how long have you been driving, "Well, I passed my test before we were married, but we were never in a position to buy a car. My Dad paid for the lessons and test as an extra wedding present, so it's certainly come in handy now, its school in the morning girls", Jane being the oldest said "we will be able to look after Trevor", Barbara said "Thank you, Jane, that's very kind of you, but it won't be for a few weeks yet" "Barbara come down in the week I don't go anywhere much" "I will Betty".

I was down at the office sharp at seven o'clock Richard turned up, have you all met one another, "Tom will you go and meet Arthur at the bottom of the downs and sort out three dozen of the older lambs run them through the weigher, take the book and chart with you, Arthur will have the dog with him, I'll meet up with you later". "Right Ted let's go and have a look at this first hedge madam would like you to tackle", first we went through a few gates, across another field and stopped at a hedge like I never seen before, there it is he said with a smile, "Have you never touched it before?" "We've only nibbled at it I'm afraid".

"Obviously she wants a good job made of it Richard", "you will certainly be in her good books if you can, well first of all there's a hell of lot to come out, there's some nice sapling oak ash and elm I can leave at different intervals, I can get some stakes from the hedge itself and also some Shoots for finishing the top off, but there will be a lot to get off".

"I never asked you about tools Ted", "Well, I've got what I want at the moment", "but you will want something to carry your tool about in so there's a small tractor in the shed for you to use whenever you want it, come back with me now I'll show you the tractor and get your tools and make a start. We will probably want your help Wednesday morning with the sheep, but I will call you if we do".

I went home collected a drink and a sandwich and the tools I wanted, I wasn't far wrong about the amount of rubbish I pulled out before I even pleached any to lay. To start with I was able to leave a nice ash sapling to start and clean out all round so they could see what it might look like. I had chucked out a number of stakes, but putting them a foot apart it's surprising how many it takes.

I sat down for a break dinner time and thought how I could work a piece work price out, but then that wouldn't work knowing that I would be wanted for other work about the farm. I had cleared about twenty five yards with an oak sapling about twenty yards if I could leave them about that all the way it would look alright.

Next morning I was out before anyone else was, and up to the hedge, I suppose I was eager to show what it would look like, I did like hedge laying. After dinner I was cleaning out some nice young Shoot for binding the top when I spotted a Landrover coming, I guessed it was Richard.

"Good afternoon Ted my goodness you've found another five yards of field and laid some", "yes I'm just getting some benders for the top". "Ted I must ask you, have you been home for dinner"? "No I bring a sandwich and a drink I've always sat down where I was". "Well, I must tell you madam won't like that, she always insists we go home for lunch", "Well, I won't argue with that, do you think she will approve of what I'm doing, it will be the first hedge laying we have ever had done for years", "I think she will be over the moon".

"Every so often she holds a little party on the big lawn for workers and a few of her friends, and she will love showing off that she is having the hedge laying done, don't be surprised if she comes out and have a has a chat with you any time".

"Is there anything you wanted Ted", "I could do with some hedge stakes as you can see I can get some out of the hedge itself", "if I get a couple of hundred when I take these lambs to market that will help you on a bit, don't forget if you want to do some overtime you're welcome to do some, and remind Barbara I'll pick her up with the others Friday morning nine o'clock. Drop your time sheet off in the office box Thursday night, the secretary will pick them up on Friday morning. Now next week we must do the shearing, I've ordered the shearers first thing Monday, that will take us the best part of next week".

Barbara had her car insurance cover come so she was able to get out more, went down to Stoke and saw nan and grandad and also great granny and grandad next door, she told nanny how she will pick her up and take her home to look after the children while she went shopping.

My brother called in unexpected Sunday and told us he was leaving, moving the next day Monday to the job he went for head forester close to Andover in Hampshire.

He wanted to know what I was doing, I told him I was hedge laying and there was a small wood I was going to sort out hazel and chestnut, well, it something we've all had our hands in handed down from Dad. He like our little car, Barbara showed it off to them she was very happy with it, Peggy said "you will be able to come down and see us now, we haven't forgot we got an agreement between us we would have Mum and Dad for a break now and then", Wally said "we're going down to see them now".

Next morning about half the sheep were rounded up ready to be filed through, Tom and John catching and you Ted rolling up and bagging, the end of the week they didn't want my help with the sheep, so I was back on the hedge laying. The weeks were slipping by, and I was well on with the hedge, one afternoon I was quite busy with some heavy stumps when I heard a voice, "good afternoon Ted", to my surprise it was her ladyship. I said "good afternoon madam", "Ted can I have a word", I dropped my tools down and went over, she stood looking at the hedge, "Ted this is absolutely wonderful, I never dreamt there was so much involved, I love the way you finish off

the top of the hedge, and left the trees ever so far apart".
"Well, there's a nice holly just up there I will leave".
"Now Ted are you getting any extra for this work", "no madam, I did try to work something out a piece work price which I have done before, but having to work on the farm it would not be fair to either of us, but don't get me wrong madam, I'm not complaining". "Well, I know Richard will want you to help on the farm from time to time, so in that case I will have a word with him and see that you will be on a bonus for this work, will you agree to that", "Thank you very much madam", "I will pop round and have a chat with Barbara one afternoon", but what I did not know when I looked round, she was stood with her camera, then walked away and back to the big house, once again it went through my mind, how the other half lived.

Trevor had started school, the two girls Jane and Susan collected him for the taxi each morning, I could see Barbara was missing her shop work, so I asked her if she would like something else to do, out of the blue she said "could we have some chickens, it will give Pauline an interest", "as soon as I see Richard I will ask him. How many are you talking about", "it won't be more than a dozen in a small pen", his answer was only if you keep it down to a dozen. Dad had a small hen house left with eight hens left, he told me he had got rid of nearly all so between us we took down the hen house and moved it back home, there was a couple of bushes which would hide it from view, but I had a feeling it was not really acceptable, no more was said about it.

I was not far from finishing the hedge one afternoon, Richard came to me I knew he wanted to say something, "I will get Tom to come and sweep all the rubbish up and take it to the bomb hole Madam won't be able to see the smoke from there. Now about these chicken Ted", "yes I gather she don't altogether like the idea", "Well, she's left it to my discretion, I explained to her that they would be confined to a small run", no more was said about it.

But I had an idea that Barbara would like, I made some nest boxes with a front flap to drop down, when one of the hens went broody we could get any kind of eggs and sit them, take them off each clutch then tether them, feed and water, and if they're good a broody take the tether off and they will get back on the eggs on their own, or be lifted back on, you could hatch any kind if it works out you can take them to market and sell them as we did with the pigs. I know what we can do, we can go down and see Tom Mortimer, he's always got ducks and geese running round his farm. I put my idea to Tom, he said "What do you want to mess about with broody hens, I tell you what I've got an old paraffin incubator in the shed come and have a look", Well, it looked alright to me, I had seen one before, "you can take that and you can have any eggs you want to hatch off then I will buy them off you, I've got a chap here can rear them on from day-olds". Barbara thought that was a good idea we made our way home, we just pulled up and right behind us was two of Tom's men, "I've got your incubator in the back, where do you want it?" I had to think quickly, "Bring it round the back and put it in the big out house" it fitted nicely in the corner, and "when you get it set up and running, Tom will send these two dozen turkey eggs up".

Barbara could not wait to get it going, I had a pretty good idea how it worked so we lit it up, the thermometer worked perfectly, "Now don't forget the eggs must be turned twice a day morning and night and the water troughs must be kept full for humidity". It wasn't long before it got to the right temperature, she asked "Can I put the eggs in now"? "You can, it's your hobby, there's a piece of paper so you can tick each time you turn them, so you won't forget".

I finished the first big hedge and was quite pleased with it, especially when Tom had cleared all the rubbish away from the hedge and showed itself off. Before I started another one I decided to have go at the Coppice, there was a nice lot of hazel just right for making sheep hurdles, first of all I had to make myself a space to work. I found a lump of wood half-moon shaped that would hold the uprights for the hurdles frame, I could picture my Dad here helping me, I had knocked down a fair bit and laid it ready for sorting. When I got home for lunch time Barbara and Pauline weren't about, I guessed where they were, I quietly looked in the outhouse and they were both sat in front of the incubator, I burst out laughing, it will be a couple of weeks yet. "Come and sit down with us, I've got your dinner here" and there were not twenty four eggs, there were thirty", "Well, you will have to take a ride down to the pet shop and get some chick boxes somewhere".

Wally sent a letter telling us all about his job and how big the estate was, he was still waiting to move into the head forester's house, and his house would come empty for me to move into if ever I thought of moving, you would certainly earn a lot more than you are at the moment, for the work you are doing.
I gathered up a sheet from the farm on my way back from to the coppice, I made sure it was it enough to work under when it's wet and outside when it's dry. Friday afternoon I was carrying a bundle of long rods back to the shelter, they would be ready for next week, I just got back to cut some more down, when Richard came through the bushes, "Hello Ted, I've found you well," "I've been here most of the week". "Tom told me he had cleared all the rubbish away and thought you had started the coppice".
"Well, I thought I would take a walk round this afternoon,

which I must admit I don't very often do, and I must say how good it looked, and here it looks as though you've you got a little industry going", "Richard I think hedges and woodland should be maintained". "Well, I know your Dad Walt was very much into this sort of work". "Well, my brother has just taken a job as head Forrester down in Hampshire, so I think he was a very good teacher".

"Which is the next hedge you want done?" "What about the one on the left as you come up the farm Drive?" "I think there is enough there for me to have a go at, the other side I see is hand clipped" "That's a low privet hedge clipped by the gardener" Richard said with a grin, "Don't think they'd have much idea how to lay a hedge".

"To save you coming to the office, Ted, I've brought your wages, now one day next week I'm going to bring Madam round, I'll walk her up the hedge and then across here and you can explain to her what you are doing she only came out once when you started, so it's time she came round, and make sure you use the little tractor", "Well, it certainly comes in handy for carrying my stuff around" "You're always out and gone in the mornings before I get to the farm, right we will see you one day next week".

When I got home Barbara said "you'll never guess who came to see me this afternoon", "No go on, tell me" "It was Madam, she had been out riding, I thought I heard a horse, she had tied it to the gate and came to the door and knocked, when I opened it", "Hello Barbara I hope it's not inconvenient me calling round" I did remember she liked to be called madam. "Madam, how nice to see you, please come in", she took her into the big lounge, "Would you like a cup of tea" "That would be very nice, thank you". When she came back in with the tea and of course some of Nanny's homemade cake, madam was looking out of the window, "Isn't it a wonderful view", we sat down and chatted. "Your little boy Trevor, he's at school now and

Pauline? "Oh she's having her afternoon nap" She wanted to know where I was born and how long we had been married, so I told her the whole story how we knew each other at school and kept together right through, how I helped my Dad on the farm where he worked and when I got married, and how you got your own pigs and then how the village started to fall apart.

It was then she said how sad and a shock it was when Mr Mason died as she knew him very well, and also how they made the film Path News, it must have been exciting, "You know, Barbara, its giving me an idea. I see you have got yourself a little car, do you drive?" "Yes I do Madam", "How wonderful, it been lovely talking to you, I will see you again shortly, bye-bye", she was on her horse and away and nothing was said about the chickens and nothing about my hobby with the incubator, well, we will carry on with that.

Pauline had just woken before you came in, "I bet you could do with your tea now". "Well, Richard came to see me this afternoon and said he's coming round to the coppice with Madam next week to let her see what I'm doing, and he also brought my pay packet to save me going to the office" "And I nearly forgot to take Pauline down to Nan's early and Trevor ready for school taxi and go shopping in the mini bus". "Well, you better look at my pay packet to see if it all been worth it, I done the Saturday morning in the coppice for a bit of overtime".

Lunch time came I asked Barbara if she would like to take a ride out on Sunday, she said "Let's go and pick up your Nan and Granddad and take them out somewhere" the children they were all for that. "Mummy said we could give them a surprise" we did bring that double bed with us we could make that up for them tonight. "Right we'll do that this afternoon and I'll keep the surprise for tomorrow", so off we go to the car, the door was soon opened by Trevor followed quickly by Pauline straight into Nanny's arms, "Where have you been?" Trevor could not keep a secret, "we've got a surprise for you", Barbara said "we would like to take you back with us and you stay the night with us and we all go out tomorrow for the day". "Have you got a bed for us?" "Yes we have, now there's no need to hurry, I will help you pack a few things". It seemed strange going to see Grandad and him not showing you his rabbits and chickens and not collecting the eggs. "Grandad, you had better bring your wellies", "What on earth will he want his wellies for?" "You will see tomorrow".

We got their case and bags inside, first thing the children was to take Nan and Grandad to the outhouse, "you must not touch it Grandad" said Pauline, "We must not touch it you tell Nanny what we have to do". "We have to turn the eggs and one day by magic we have some baby chicks", so then Barbara told them the whole story, "Ted's found an infrared lamp so when they have hatched we put them with a little bit of food and water and when they're all dry box them up and take them down to Mr Mortimer and he is willing to pay Barbara and it won't cost us anything. I tick the bit of paper so I don't forget I've turned them".

Next morning we packed some food for a picnic, took a couple of flasks of hot water to make a cup of tea and a drink for the children and off we went. Trevor kept saying "Are we there Dad have we got far to go?" I stopped along the road, what can you see, "Nanny it's the sea"! "Walt, you know where we are, it's been a long time since we've been down here, it's Bosham Harbour, you'll see all the boats in a minute and then we can go winkle picking and get some cockles and take them back to eat". We parked the car in a nice spot along the harbour, we sat down under the harbour wall and Ted and Grandad went winkle picking with Trevor, there isn't a lot of sand but we had a nice spot and we had a very nice day out, then the time came to pack up and make for home which did not go down very well with the children.

Well into next week, I had put a few hurdles by which I already had made, put the frame ready to start another and had the pleaching post which was growing from a stump and a number of piles of different sizes, cane and pieces of wood. I heard someone calling back at the shelter, I thought I'm not going to go back empty handed', so another bundle went back to the shelter, and who was sitting down but Richard and Madam. "Richard I never expected to see anything like this!" she came across to me, "Ted, can you show me exactly what you are doing?" "Well, Madam, that's the frame where I start the hurdle, if you stand well back you will see why, so I put the end of the rod in, twist it through the pegs, go to the end and give it a twist. It flew back over my head to come back across the frame again, remembering to leave a gap so the shepherd can put a post through and carry about half a dozen at a time".

"Wow" she said "I can see you don't want anybody too close. Richard, did you see that?" "Yes Madam, I did". "Now Madam, some of the rods are too thick and have to be split, so I put this old leather boot leg on my arm, split the end with my hook, push it on to my arm". Showing her how it was done. "Now they're ready to use. This post is of no use in the same sort of way, only for big fencing rails, I split the end with an axe, open it up with a wooden wedges and push it on to the post pegs each side", showing her exactly how it was done. "Ted I think it's absolutely fantastic! I have never seen it done before. Richard, can I have a word?" They went off for a bit and came back, "Ted, I remember you telling me a film crew came to Masons Farm once, I have an idea. I have a friend who loves filming and does it for a living, will you be kind enough to allow him to make a film of your work?" Jokingly I looked at Richard and said "At this rate I will be asking for film star money?" and she said quickly, "You will be doing it in your work time", so I said "Providing he don't want me swinging from tree to tree and eat nuts and leaves!" "Now Ted, don't be silly, I think it's absolutely fascinating what you're doing. Richard will give you all the details later, thank you very much" and off they went.

I went home one night leaving the incubator to Barbara to look after, "Daddy come and have a look", they went to turn the eggs as usual and looking through the glass in the door six or eight had hatched and some were chipped, "Mummy put the heater on which was on the floor with sawdust chippings". "Well, I suggest we have our tea first and then we sort them out after, there may be a few more then", Well, tea did not take long off we went to the outhouse, "I will lift them down Mummy can take them and put them under the lamp", she let the children hold one or two with great excitement. There was ten and still more to come and already they were pecking at the crumbs and water, "We will let them settle and see them again before we go to bed".

We sat in the garden and talked, Barbara said "Daddy's got something to tell you" "These little chicks that are hatching out, they don't belong to us", and then came the questions, "you know the man who bought our pigs, Well, they're his eggs and he's paying Mummy to hatch them out and when they're ready to go Mummy will box them up and take them back to him to carry on looking after them, these are turkey chicks but we don't know what the next ones will be".

Before we went to bed there was ten more hatched out, Ted said "It looks as though most of them might be out before dinner tomorrow and then you can take them the following day and collect your money". "We never talked about money" she said, "I might be able to do a bit of wheeling and dealing with him".

I started on the hedge at the bottom of the Drive which was a nice one to do, not much to cut out, nice long Shoots to lay almost like making a hurdle. The taxi went by with the children to school waving merrily, next to come was Barbara, "I'm taking the chicks down to Tom Mortimer" she could not wait to see how much he was going to give her, she told me he was in the yard when she got there. "Good morning Mrs Rogers, have you got something for me?" "Yes, I've got your first batch of chicks" "Let's have a look at them", she said there was thirty eggs twenty eight hatched and two dud. "If I give you seven pounds fifty how does that sound?" "Round it up to eight, Mr Mortimer, that would sound a lot better" "Well, being as they're turkey chicks, I will do that".

"Can you take a hundred chicken eggs?" "Ted said we could get hundred chicken eggs in", before I looked round, his man took the box with the chicks and handed her the trays of a hundred eggs. She came home cleaned the incubator and set it going, and had it filled with eggs again.

A letter came from Wally and Peg saying if I change my mind, the job with him is still open, but I could not see us moving just yet, but I said that feeling was on the agenda one day.

That day the head gardener came across the Drive, I had not met him yet, straight away he said, "I understand you're cutting out some rustic poles for me, I want them soon", I snapped back and said, "When the manager talks to me, I will get them, and won't be the best sticks you will get. If her ladyship wants the woodlands in good shape it will be the best kept to grow on". "Oh we will see about that" and walked off, he was lucky a piece of wood did not follow him.

That afternoon Richard did come to me, "Ted, next time you go down to the coppice, will you cut out some rustic poles for the gardener?" I said "The next time you see him tell him to keep away from me" "He hasn't been out and upset you as well? I don't know why her ladyship keeps him on" "When I have cut them out, someone can come and fetch it, I am going to finish this hedge first".

Our second Christmas was coming up and again we were invited with the children to the big house for a party, it was never a party for us, it was where she could show off to her friends, you were called to go up to Father Christmas and get your present, which was an envelope with half a week's wages and the bonus was nothing like I was promised, and Barbara had given up on hatching any more eggs for Tom, so he took the incubator back.

Neither of us was really happy with the situation, especially when they came up with the idea that they may start to charge workers house rent. Barbara and I had talked about Wally's request to go and work with him, but the house situation had not been sorted yet, Barbara wrote to them and said we were thinking about it, he wrote back immediately to go down and see them, which we did a month later.

He showed me the set up, I would be earning a lot more money working alongside him, he was still waiting for the old Head Forester to move so he could go in his house, but we were prepared to go into the house they offered us, if they did some improvements. He had a word with his Boss and he accepted the fact that the two of us working together was good for the estate.

Great day at Linley

Left to right
 Antony Perry, Ted, Tom Parry and John Blackburn in December 1979

Barbara walked the pheasant laying pens and collected the eggs ready to put in the incubator for hatching

See story Pages 70 and 196

Chapter 6

The Second Move

I gave my notice in, much to the upset and surprise but Richard understood. Madam could not have cared less, I felt I had really worked for nothing, but I knew I will be earning nearly double the money.

Soon after we moved, Barbara was approached at the school about fostering children, Pauline had started school, she asked me about it and said there was a lot of children needed looking after. Social worker called round, "Can you have a little one tomorrow?"

It was a good job we had got our little car, Barbara had to take the children to school and fetch them home at night, some old enough to go to school, some had clothes some not, so Barbara found herself going to jumble sales, it was a good job I was earning good money.

It was certainly not for the fostering money, it was because she loved the children, but the house was becoming a problem, my brother was chasing the Boss every week, he said there was nothing he could do until the old man moved, and Wally went into his house and I had Wally's house.

Over two years had gone by, Barbara was getting unsettled, she put her arms around me when I got home one night and told me she was expecting another baby, I said I did not want her to have any more foster children at that moment, my sister in law was very good, she visited Barbara every day to help.

I talked to Wally about different things, he said I will make a promise to you, if you leave for another job, I will always want you to come back here and work with me, we shook hands. But it won't be yet for a while, I want to earn a lot more money first, we did work well together.

Time went by and Barbara had a baby boy a little earlier than expected, but everything went well with Peggy and the midwife there, the doctor arrived. Soon, after couple of days and she was up and about as usual Peggy still came, I think she was pleased to have the company. The baby Colin Nigel was growing and started moving around, we decided to look round for another job, but it wasn't easy. I applied for job at Pendock on the Gloster Ledbury road, he replied to my letter, it said he was coming to Andover and would call in and see us. We decided the job was more or less the same as I had been doing, Barbara asked about the house and he suggested we go and see him at his place the following weekend.

Wally knew all about this, we went up and had a look, the house was a lot better than the one we had, it was close to the school, on a regular bus route. I met the manager, it was a job of all sorts. I would not always know what I was doing on each morning, it was very much a mixed farm, the money was not as much as I was getting, but there was a lot of overtime to be had.

I agreed to take the job, and a van would move us in a fortnight, I gave Wally my notice and it was not easy, but he could see my position, we promised to keep in touch. Peggy said "We will come and see you when you're settled in".

Chapter 7

Third move to Pendock

First job I had was a lot of fencing post and rails round the horse paddocks, I did not know they had horses. Weeks went by when I had the job to take the tractor and trailer load of manure to the walled garden at the Boss's house and was in the yard, I had not met her yet and she said "I want it over there" I did not see the small car parked, she beckoned me back, then suddenly stopped me, I then got out and walked to the back and the small car was slightly hooked onto the trailer. Just then the gardener came through the gate and was not very pleased, "What you are going to do about that" "I can lift it off", which I did. There was not a scratch on it.

He could not believe what I did, I did not blame him for being upset, she said "John, take it to the garage now and get it checked over, we will sort it out" "John is it" "Ted I'm sorry about this, but I cannot see a mark on it, take it down to the garage now". "Did she back you onto my car" "Yes she did" "Well, you will soon find out she's nuts". He moved the car and I was able to empty the trailer.

I met up with him a few days later and he was happy that there wasn't a scratch on it, so we shook hands and introduced ourselves properly, Ted Rogers, John Blackburn, and my wife's name is Dorrie said John.

I also went down to the garage with the idea of looking for a bit bigger car, I done a deal, swapped our little car, with some cash, we were sad to see it go, but we realised with the children growing up we needed a bigger car.

The local school had a kind of youth club but adults were invited, so we met there a number of times and became very good friends. He loved fishing and said he would like to get into Game keeping, which seemed very strange because that was my way of thinking.

We both got friendly with a local Game Keeper and I very quickly learned a few tricks of the trade, I must say I did not go along with some of them, but I kept them in my head.

I also got friendly with the local bobby Doug Tully and I joined as a special constable, Barbara was also involved with the school and talked of how we were foster parents, not knowing that one of the women was a social worker, she asked Barbara if she would consider doing it again, jokingly she said, "Ted and I always said we had two boys and a girl. If we had another one of our own we would like a girl, a sister for Pauline.

She looked at Barbara and said "if I brought you out a little baby girl tomorrow, it would be a long term arrangement", "I have a lot of baby clothes, can you come in the evening when Ted's home" "Yes of course I can, about half past six", Barbara said "I look forward to that".

When I got home she was all smiles, I said what are you so happy about, she said "we are going to have a baby sister for Pauline", and she said "I've got a lovely feeling about this one". She told Pauline how she was going to have a sister, and of course sorted baby clothes out she kept saying, "I wonder how big she is, I've got two bottles and nappies, I wonder what milk she's on, or she might be on solid food". I said "Barbara calm down you're like a broody hen running round!" "Well, it's a while since I had a little one".

You know what I did this afternoon? Go and look in the bedroom, I did and there on the cupboard was a nice cradle, I said "Where did you get that from?" "I went across to the shop to get a paper and on the board was a ticket,

'For Sale a baby's cradle' and it was just down the road. We have seen the woman at the school, so I went and knocked on the door she was very pleased to see me. "We have met at the school, its June isn't it? I'm Barbara", "Come in" "Yes of course I can help" "Well, I've called about the cradle". She looked at me a bit old fashioned, "it's alright, I'm not expecting, well I am tonight, I've got a little one coming who we're going to look after". "It's in the bedroom, it was my daughter's cradle but she no longer needs it".

"How much did she want for it?" Barbara coughed, "It was very clean, she would like five pounds for it", I said "Okay, can I take it now" "If you can manage it", so I gave her five pounds and carried it home, "Is that alright!" Ted said "Of course it is, if that's what you want", she said "I've got a nice feeling about this".

We had finished tea and cleared away, a car pulled up, Barbara opened the door and two women stood there, one had a bag with a few things in, the social worker had a shawl and the baby was small, you could hardly see it. "Hello Barbara, here's your little baby", I quickly called them in, Barbara took the baby, "Isn't she small!" she sat down, Pauline was right there by her side, "Is that my little sister" "Yes" said Mum "Isn't she lovely?" the boys carried on playing with their toys.

"How old is she" "She is six weeks old. We have brought a small tin of milk powder and a bottle", "I've got two bottles, I wasn't sure" "Have you got a cradle for her?" "Yes I bought one this afternoon". One of them said "We must be going Barbara, and we will pop round next week just to see how you're getting on", they said their goodbyes and went.

John came by and took Trevor fishing which he loved doing, it seemed incredible how fast the children were growing up, Dorrie also called by to take Pauline to

Church which she did quite regularly, but a good excuse to see our new addition to the family. They also had a boy and girl of their own, they chatted on how they knew John and I was keen on one day getting a Keeper's job.

Dorrie was nursing the baby and suddenly Barbara popped the question, if we had her christened, "Would you and John like to be her god parents? We have already decided on a name it will be Patricia Mary Rogers. I will make enquiries first to the council through the social worker" "Oh Barbara, you have made my day, John will be thrilled".

The phone had been on for a week which meant we were able to contact Wally and Peggy. He gave me a ring saying Mum had not been very well, and they had moved them lock stock and barrel up to his place, and Mum was feeling a bit better, Dad was messing about in the woods doing his thing, and they will come up and see us shortly.

I said I will give you a ring with maybe a surprise, we got a reply saying there was no problem and we go ahead with the christening, brother and sister Mum and Dad and their two girls came up and we had a lovely day.

My sister rang saying she had an Alsatian dog puppy she could not control would I be interested, she brought it up one day, I had always liked dogs, this one especially I took to and so did the children.

I also got friendly with the local bobby Doug Tully. PC Tully called in one night and asked me to walk round the village, each time I went out, I rang in the office and when I came home. Roma was his wife's name, he just wanted a lot of attention. Social life was quite good which Barbara enjoyed, one I was very much involved with, was tug of war, and there was a lot of commotion with that.

Wally rang one day, he had some bad news, our Mum had passed away. Our friend Dorrie offered to come and live at our house and look after the children for a couple of

days. The reaction I got from the Boss' you will have to take it off your holiday', (more likely from his wife.)
When we got back from the funeral, Dorrie and John were pleased to see us and everything was alright, John told us he was on the look-out for a Keeper's job but no luck yet, I said I may be doing the same, but I was not going to rush into moving, the children were growing up even faster, Pauline and Tricia were inseparable.

Tragedy...

There was an old man who used to walk about the village asking people for a pound, so he could get a pint from the pub including Barbara. All refused him. Doug called in that evening and asked me to walk out with him, he got a call on his radio, this man was found by a farmer laying in a cattle water trough in his yard. Doug put me on guard at the farm gate, while he took control. It was a bit early, police and ambulance came and it was quickly cleared and brought to a close.
One day, the Boss's wife walked by and spotted the dog in the garden with Barbara and called out to her, "You must get rid of that animal" I told Doug about it, and he said "I can verify the dog is safe, I see enough of him". When I told the manager, I told him, "I wasn't going to put up with that from her", I was talking to John he said how stupid she was, she was with him in the garden.
I was trimming a hedge alongside the road one day she went by me and shouted back, "If you don't like it here you can go", I shouted back "Don't worry, I will go when I'm ready". But she was like that with all workers, it was not a nice place to live or work, we both agreed we would carry on and keep looking for another job.

The two work horses Jock and Silver Ted worked with when he worked on a farm in his early days.

See story page 21

Chapter 8

Interview Portleesh Ireland.

Barbara was looking through the Shooting Times magazine, first of two adverts, Keepers wanted urgently, Portleesh, Southern Ireland Jokingly, she said "ring up" I plucked up courage and rang that night, I was amazed some one answered. Lord D——, I said "Good evening, sir I understand you are looking for a Game Keeper", "Yes I am, where are you speaking from?" I told him where we were and our address and phone number.

"May I come and see you tomorrow? I have someone to meet over there, I can catch the ferry this evening, I think I will be with you just after lunch time". It so happened it was Saturday, he seemed to be in a bit of a rush and put the phone down.

I did some work in the morning. Barbara said "We had better be ready just in case he turns up" To my surprise a Land Rover pulled up, I was talking to the local PC, a gentle-man jumped out "I'm looking for Mr Rogers", Doug said "This is the man you want", he shook my hand, "I'm Lord D———" "Shall we go in the house?" I said, "This is my wife", he shook hands, "I may sound in a bit of a hurry, but I do need someone quickly, my estate is on the main road, south of Port Leash you can't miss it, it's the only gateway with big iron gates and lions heads on the posts".

"Now, when do you think you will be able to come and see our home?" "Well, it won't be until next Saturday we can catch the ferry from Holyhead to Dublin first thing in the morning and should be with you before lunch" "I will give you some money for your fare and car. Well, I look forward to meeting you next Saturday", he shook hands

and got in his Land Rover and was away.
 Doug was still outside, "Who was that, Ted" I laughed and said "Lord —— he's just offered me a job in southern Ireland and left me some money for the fare next Saturday" "Well, even if you go there's nothing to say you've got to take the job", so we decided to give it a go. Barbara phoned the ferry company, ordered and paid for the tickets and got them in the week. I said I would ask John and Dorrie if they will sit again, I told him what we're doing, he said "You must be mad, of course we will come and look after the house for you, but I hope you don't take it". "No I probably won't, but it will give us a day out and see what Ireland is like".
We caught the early ferry and made our way down through Southern Ireland, although there had been some political trouble there, until we came to a place called Port Leash. Barbara said "I wonder what all those people are queuing up for", "I said I don't know", it was not long before we went by some big iron gates. "That must be the place back there."
I turned round and there were the lions on the posts. I drove slowly up, the Drive looked a bit of a mess, there was a chap walking down the Drive, I stopped and asked him if this was Lord D----place, "what have you come for?" "I said I've come for an interview for the Game Keeper's job", he laughed and walked off.
The big house did not look very impressive, I knocked on the door. A woman came, but did not say who she was, I said who we were, "Have you come for an interview with his lordship? I'm afraid you're out of luck, he's been taken to hospital. I can take you round for a look at the estate", she still did not say who she was.
I was not very impressed with what I saw, I could see Barbara was not very happy. Back at the house we got out, she pointed across the yard, "the house that goes with the

job is over there, it's open, so go and have a look", we went in, it was the worst house eve. Barbara grabbed my hand and said "Let's go home."
Back in the yard, the woman was waiting, she said "I suppose he gave you money to cover your expenses", and still never said who she was and went back in the house. We agreed to phone the ferry to see if we can get on one soon in the afternoon, we were lucky there was plenty of room. Barbara was not a very good sailor so she had taken a tablet for sea sickness, I'm glad she had it, it was not a very smooth crossing and slept most of the way back.
What a story we had to tell them, John and Dorrie could hardly believe what we told them.

Second advert and interview…

What we wanted. Trevor would soon be leaving school, Colin not far behind, Tricia had started school.
The second advert was for a new syndicate stating 'No hatching, will buy in poults for release pens, barn conversion bungalow, three bedrooms Markgate Dunstable.' I immediately rang the phone number and fixed a meeting with the Shoot Boss.
I was glad I got a bigger car because it was quite a long way to go, we made enquiries in Markgate and found it was up a fairly good back road at a farm which was owned by two old gentlemen who had nothing to do with the Shoot, but rented it to the syndicate.
We drove into the yard and there was two old gentlemen sitting on a bench, I walked over to them, they said "Are you the chap that's come for the interview?" I said "Yes" and introduced myself and Barbara, "I'm John and he's Harry, well, he's just rung to say he's on his way", one of them said "I see you've got a young family, have you had a long Drive?" "Yes we have" "Well, let them have a run

round I will get our sister to bring out some tea", she came out with tea and drinks for the children, looked at her brother John and said "This will liven the place up a bit!"

Just then a big impressive car drove into the yard, a man got out and came straight to us and apologised for being late and thanked Lilly and her brothers for looking after us, "I will see you before I go, John. Now Mr. Rogers and Mrs, very pleased to meet you, come into the house. Mrs Rogers would you like to have a look round? As you can see, it's a bungalow, we rent it off the farm, we pay the rent for the phone, and you pay for the calls".
"This coming season will be the first one as a syndicate proper, we will buy in the poults, we have the woods, we will want you to decide where to put the release pens. There does seem to be a number of wild birds, and there's the pond, we would like to encourage wild duck, we have a good flight line. We have an old Land Rover which is good enough for field work, but not road worthy. If it needs work on it, it goes to my garage for repairs. Your children are growing up" "Yes they are" "Well, before we go any further, my name is George and you are Ted and Barbara".
I said "Well, Barbara, what do you think of this house?" "We have not had a bungalow before", "but I like it very much", "Now Ted, how about the job?" "I think I could do a good job here" George said "Well, it's coming up to Christmas. Is there any hurry to start before?" "No the beginning of January will be all right" "Let me look at my diary". We went back to his car, "How about the fifth of January?" "Yes that will be alright" "Give me your address and phone number, here's my card, and there will be a vehicle on that morning. Now if I give you fifty pounds that will cover your expenses for today" I said "Thank you very much" and we shook hands, wished each

other a happy Christmas and made our way back home. With fifty pounds extra in our pocket we could afford to stop on the way home for something to eat. On the way, the children very soon fell asleep. Barbara and I were talking all the way, I collected the dog from John and told him where we had been, I said we will see you later and tell you all about it.

I gave my notice in and told the manager I would be leaving on the fifth of January. Just then the Bosses wife came in the yard "Haven't you got any work to do" "Ted has just given me his notice" "Oh that's good" she said, "You won't be wanting your Christmas box then will you?" I politely told her what she could do with her Christmas box and quickly retreated out of the yard, the manager just laughed and I carried on washing the dairy.
We met up with John and Dorrie at the school club one night and had a good chat, he said he had applied for a Keeper's job in Norfolk, but had not had a reply yet. We saw the social worker and said we would like to have a chat, and she asked if she could come and visit and was told she can come in the evening and see us all as a family. She came and we explained the situation and she came across this problem with agricultural workers, but I said, "We also try to improve our standard of living which we have, and there is one other thing we would like you to take on for us, we desperately want to adopt Tricia" She said, "I don't see any problem with that at all and I am very pleased to hear that, give me your future address and phone number, you have mine. If I don't see you before, have a nice Christmas and a happy New Year and I will be in touch, isn't your dog well, behaved? He hasn't moved all the time I've been here!" I said "He's one of the family".
We both spoke to Wally and Peggie over Christmas and

had a long chat, he said when my house is free there will be a job here for you when you want it, and maybe we will come up and see you one weekend.

Trevor got a job on a farm part-time under a mechanic which was what he wanted, he loved messing about with engines, and Barbara took Pauline, Tricia and Colin to school and back each day.

Ted as a single-handed Keeper at Linley with John Blackburn, Keeper on the neighbouring Lyndham Estate in December 1979

Chapter 9

Fourth move to Markgate

We moved to Markgate on the fifth of January, first thing I did was have a go at the vermin and there was plenty of that at Christmas. I treated myself to a twelve bore shot gun and got a licence, that came in handy, plus I was working out where to put the release pens, it seemed acceptable to George, I asked him if he had a Shoot room, he said "Why?" I said "It will be somewhere for your guns to meet in the morning and to have lunch and back to at night" "Well, that's something we had not thought about, sounds like a good idea" "There is a loose box, we could ask John if we could clean it up and make use of it and if someone had a wood burner to give, and there's my garage I can use for the Beaters"

"Ted I'm going to call a syndicate meeting and put all this to them", I had no say in the money side of the Shoot, some of them knew how a Shoot day was organised but some had no idea and was quite surprised when I spelt it out to them, especially the safety side of it.

They agreed to buy four thousand poults, a brace of birds to each gun, the rest sold to a Game dealer. First lot of birds came, Barbara helped me release them in one pen, the second lot came the next day for the other pen, I made sure there was plenty of perching for them, because I knew it was well known for them to crowd up in a corner and suffocate. This meant late night patrolling and this is where Roma came in for a guard dog and he was good.

I later found out there was a group from Hamel Hampstead going round different Shoots, poaching whatever they could get their hands on. I gathered a few lads from the village for beating, the men turned up in their Land

Rovers and big cars. They liked the idea of a Shoot room, I showed George where I wanted his him to take his team down the side of the wood, they had made a draw so each gun knew which peg to go to, I had already pegged each Drive the day before.

I had started feeding the birds out to a small spinney in the field. I could see they were ready and before we started each Drive, I would blow my whistle, my order to the Beaters was to take it slowly and no dog running ahead and no shouting.

The birds went out high over the guns, a lot of banging and not a lot of birds down, we picked up and moved on to the next Drive which was a bit better, lower birds, but bad in skill of sportsmanship, left the high birds and more or less blew the lower birds to pieces, I mentioned this to George, "Don't worry, it's exactly what I want", but I could see one or two never had a clue what it was all about.

Towards the end of the season, those one or two were complaining there was not enough birds in the bag which I was not happy to hear, and replied back saying, "If you learned to Shoot properly there would be", I was backed up by George and some of the others.

But somehow I could see how it was going, back in the early days when we got interest in the Keepering job, I joined the Game Keepers association and it was very much like a bush telegraph, you went to the Game Fairs and met a number of Keepers. You often swapped ideas and phone numbers, sometimes you got a call from someone short of a picker up, 'can you give us a day on a certain day,' and you did because you never knew when you might need some help yourself.

The police were keen on catching a group that were wanted for other crimes also. I was woken one night about one o'clock I could hear Roma giving a part howl and whining, I knew something was wrong, Barbara was awake, I told her I was taking the dog, don't worry. I heard a couple of shots, I knew exactly where it was close to one of the release pens. I knew the dog wouldn't bark unless I tell him to speak. I could hear voices, I always carried a good stick with me which I was prepared to use. Suddenly I heard sticks cracking and guessed they were moving. I shouted "Police stop where you are" The dog was getting excited, I gave him a bit longer lead, I gave the word speak, I have never seen him so vicious, as luck would have it they were running down the Drive-way which lead out on to a hard road.

I did not know that a police car was parked in the gateway, they heard me and the dog, they were waiting to see what was happening, when two men ran out straight into the arms of the law, I followed out and recognised one of the PC's, "Hello Ted", with the two in handcuffs.

"Well, that went very well thanks a lot, Ted, we will be round to see you later", they were impressed how the dog reacted, he had calmed down by now and back home, a good nights work. I learned later that those two caught were involved in other crimes than poaching.

Towards Christmas, George told me two guns had pulled out of the syndicate because they could not afford it, and things were not going how he had hoped it would, although there was a lot of birds left. He asked me if I would walk round with him and two others to help pay my wages and other things.

This I could not really believe was happening, I said if you are as desperate as that, why not Shoot so many, help me put up some small pens and feed them into them and sell birds as good un-shot for more money, he was all for that, but still walked the boundaries.

I also got friendly with the local bobby Doug Tully. PC Tully called in one night and asked me to walk round the village

I became a "Special" constable

Ted as a "Special" in police uniform with his dog Roma. Around 1979
See story page 90

Chapter 10

Our fifth Move to Lillington Darrel

Trevor had met up with a mate he had met a long time ago, Alec Morris. His parents rented a small farm on an estate in Buckinghamshire, his mate invited him home one week end and consequently he was asked if he would like a live in job on the farm. It was close to Silverstone race track, which suited both boys. He moved over there and promised he would keep in touch, we had a nice letter from Alec's mother and said he had settled in alright and the boys was good mates.

A few weeks later Trevor, rang to our surprise and said he had been talking to the agents for the estate and they said how they were looking for someone to work in the woods and also help the retiring Game Keeper with a view of taking over. He told them that was the sort of job we would be interested in. They phoned Dad and asked him to come for an interview at the estate office at Lillington Dayrell close to Buckingham, this was on the Saturday morning.

I phoned my Aunty Nell, my mother's youngest sister who was always ringing us and was always saying how they would love to see us. I thought this was an opportunity, I rang and asked if she and her husband Reg would like to stay with us for the weekend, she was over the moon 'can we come up on Friday afternoon?', Barbara spoke to her, "Yes of course you can we haven't seen you for a long time, we will a lot to talk about" I knew Roma would be alright, she loved dogs. Eleven o'clock appointment so, we had to get away early in the morning, she had never met Tricia and thought her and Pauline were well matched.

We were in good time the agent assured us they were very

wealthy family, the Boss was a gentleman banker but loved his Shooting and it was a private Shoot all guests. There was always some woodland work to do, tree felling and such like, now Tom the Keeper has moved to a bungalow, but still want to do a little bit, I said I am sure that won't be a problem.

"Now Mrs Rogers the house is empty so would you like to see it?" "Yes I would thank you" "Jump in my car and we will go down and have a look". We went about half a mile down the road and turned into a big gate-way, followed a well-kept track and suddenly an old worldly cottage loomed up out of a clearing with a little brook running through the garden fed from two lakes.

Barbara said "Isn't that beautiful!" The garden backed onto parkland, and for her, it ticked all the boxes, we came out and up the big Drive which went past a very big house that used to be the family home, but it has been very well done into a girls school for about twenty years.

We carried on through, stopped at some buildings and a yard. "This is where your workshop and saw bench is, and in future you will be asked to saw out timber for the farm. Now the manager is not here at the moment, you won't be responsible to him but there will be times he will ask for something or other.

Now I must tell you, they have three young boys which they wish to bring up as young gentlemen and learn the etiquette of Shooting. Ted and Barbara, I would like to make an appointment for you to meet the Boss and the family on Wednesday next, at eleven o'clock", I made sure he meant this next Wednesday, "one more thing you will be paid classed as a personal servant, and so your money will be paid into your bank account each week, but he will tell you more about that when you meet him. I know he will be seeing someone also at ten o'clock so don't be late, when you go out onto the main road it's the big house opposite the name plate on the gate Dayrell House". We shook hands and he wished us good luck and said "I will see you again shortly as if we knew we would get the job. I will give you a ring on Tuesday evening to confirm, at six o'clock", he gave us a wave goodbye.

As we came out onto the main road Barbara said "slow down, that must be the big house Dayrell House, wow", I laughed and said "Do you want to Drive?" and she said "I will when I'm over the shock". About half way and she took over the wheel, we got home not too late, the children and the dog were pleased to see us and said it's been a wonderful day, and Pauline and Tricia both at the same time said, "Where do you think we've been?" and both together "We went to the zoo at Dunstable" "Well, that was very kind of Aunty and Uncle".

But now we've got something to ask them, now Nell said "what's that", Barbara asked quietly, "How long can you stop, would you like to stop all the week" "Oh Barbara do you mean that?" turning to Reg, "I'm Game?, he said "But why!" asked Nell, Ted butted in "Well, you will be doing us a big favour, we have another interview on Wednesday and we will get a phone call six o'clock on Tuesday", and then of course we had to tell them the whole story. We could not believe the last time we saw them was at Mum's funeral her sister Edith.

The two girls thought it was wonderful to have Aunty and Uncle stopping with us they were being spoilt, we had tea and Barbara and I sat by the phone holding hands, Nell laughed, "This one must be special, let us take the children in the other room". Dead on six o'clock the phone rang, "Is that Ted Rogers?" "Yes it is" I said "As I promised your interview is still on for eleven o'clock tomorrow with Mr Clark at Dayrell house".

Colin said, "Are we going to move again Dad?" he said "I hope we will know for sure tomorrow". Up early next morning, Nell had obviously rehearsed the children. They lined up at the door and gave us a kiss for good luck Mum and Dad.

We arrived early, got to the door dead on eleven o'clock Barbara stood with me, another car pulled up just as the door opened, the other chap I thought. We stood on the step together, he looked at me and asked who I was, "Mr and Mrs Rogers sir an appointment at eleven o'clock", he looked at the other chap, I didn't quite catch his name, "10 o'clock my appointment" straight away he said "you are late you can go, Mr and Mrs Rogers you come in please". We went into a very posh room, Mr Clark said, "this is my wife", she said, "I'm so pleased he brought you as well,", "I am Grandma", a voice came from a chair in the corner, "we have three boys, when they're at home I very much want them to know the way the estate works and especially the Shooting, as you know Tom the Keeper is retiring. I would like more birds reared. If you want more help, I will see you get it", she butted in, "Mrs Rogers, if I came to you one day and asked can you look after my youngest son Jamie, he's four", Barbara explained how we had been foster parents.

"I understand you undertake tree felling and tree surgery", I forgot I had left my special

police badge in my lapel, he spotted it, "may I ask what the badge is", I told him I was a part time special constable, "and if you get this job will you join our force", "I most certainly will", "good" he replied, he walked across to his wife, and whispered between themselves, she looked a lot younger than him, she nodded her head in agreement, he came back, shook my hand, "Rogers I'd like to offer you the job and Mrs Rogers I hope to see you again in the near future". His wife shook hands "have a safe journey back". He said "I will instruct the agent to get in touch with you straight away and fix removals, I gather you will be paid well above the agricultural wage, classed as an agricultural worker but you will be a personal servant, you have a bank account", "yes sir I have Nat West", "that's better still, that's my bank, as I said the agent will be in touch", his wife saw us to the door and gave us a very warm goodbye.

We could not get home quick enough to tell them our news, we got the job.

Next morning I saw Richard and gave him my notice, he didn't seem at all surprised, "I would like to have a couple more days Shooting", I said "of course I will", Reg was pleased I asked him to come. On the first day he walked with me most of the time, on Friday they got ready to go home in the morning, they were so pleased we had asked them to come, we will let you know when we have got settled, Nell said please keep in touch, we promised and they were on their way.

This was our fifth move to Lillington Dayrell, the agent rang and I agreed the day, I finished they would send a furniture van, they would load some that night and slept in it, Barbara made sure they had a meal and drinks, so they got a good start in the morning. Our house was called the 'gas house' because years ago they made gas there for the estate, but all tanks and pipes were gone, when we arrived.

In the yard, waiting, the agent had told me the keys will be left in the porch, first thing Barbara did was make a cup of tea for everyone. The men soon had the doors open and started to carry furniture and tools in to where Barbara and I wanted them. As I looked around I found there was several buildings round the back of the house which will come in handy.

I had to get out and about and get to know a few people, I was staggered to see how well the estate was equipped with machinery, I went to the office and introduced myself to the farm manager John Cook, I asked him how he felt about sowing a patch of pheasant cover, he didn't think there would be a problem. I walked back to the wood yard, the big saw bench looked alright, there were no chain saws; that was something they would have to buy. I hoped I would get a Land Rover, I eventually found Tom Dodd in his bungalow not that far from our house, asked him how he felt about me more or less taking over from him.

His wife Betty said she was pleased he was retiring because they wanted more things done, Tom was not into tree work, he only had a few broody hens hatching eggs, I said "Well, the rearing side will be completely different, I will be making boxes which will hold a hundred day old poults under gas heaters from bottles and then releasing them in large pens in the woods".

I got a message from the big house one morning, would I come up and meet the butler, I met him he was quite worried about the log shed, I said "What's the matter?" "He said they're getting a bit low on logs", just then the granny came out, "Good morning, Ted", I said "Good morning Madam" "No, no, I would like you to call me 'grandma'" she said "the Boss left a message; could I catch you and explain that he would like you to keep the log shed topped up' as you can see there are some big logs" "It looks as though you could do with some this week, I will look round and see if I can find a fallen tree", I suddenly remembered I had got a saw, so I called in the office and asked the manager about it, this is something the Boss had not thought about. "The agents are not about now for a fortnight so what I can do, I can give you a ticket, go into Watsons they'll have anything you want".

He said "By the way, you cannot be expected to run your car, what you need is a Land Rover and trailer, I will get the farm manager to sort the right one out for you. If I cannot get hold of the Boss tonight I will see that you get one tomorrow". I thought I had better make my way home, Barbara will be wondering where I'd got to.

When I told her where I had been, I showed her the ticket, I had got to go and get the saws I wanted and the Land Rover I might get in the morning, it seemed as though I'm my own Boss.

As I got to know the area, I found there was a number of Shooting estates quite close by, true to his word next morning I was about to go walking, when across the field came a Land Rover and in the yard the manager jumped out, "There you are Ted this is yours, and when you need petrol, here's the key to the tank at the farm, always make sure you lock it up afterwards, the trailer will be ready tomorrow, pick it up in the afternoon. I can get a lift back on a tractor, I've got to see someone who's doing a job just across the fields", he called out to Barbara, "Is everything alright?" "Yes thank you" she replied.

In the evening there had been so much going on, the children had started to settle down and asking questions even Barbara and I were asking ourselves questions like how did we get here, where money was no problem and at last things were going our way.

I had met a few Keepers and got a lot of information. I knew I had got to get a gun dog, I met up with a local farmer one day, he did a lot of Shooting. Tom Parry, asked him if he knew where I might pick up a good pup, "Well, look no further, it so happens my Labrador bitch has had a litter, she had eight and I got two left, a dog and a bitch, but I kept them on because I rather liked them, would you be interested?" "How old are they?" "They're six months" "Well, I would like to look at the dog, how much will you take for him?" he said "You come and look at him first", he told me where, he lived at Silverstone. "Will Sunday morning do?" he smiled and said, "I don't think I will be going to church!"

I asked Barbara if she would like a ride out, "Yes, why not" Pauline was soon leaving school and this would be first time we have left her with Colin and Tricia on their own, but I knew we would not be long because Silverstone bordered the estate, we got in the Land Rover, Barbara said "isn't this posh", it was a very nice feeling.

We found Tom's farm, "Hello my dear, come and meet the wife, now would you like a cup of tea or something a bit stronger?" The ladies introduced themselves, Barbara and Margaret, I said "We will have a cup of tea please", Tom said "You ladies have a chat Ted and me will go outside with our cuppa and do business".

He let the dogs out and straight away the dog came to me, I always knew I had a way with dogs, he sat at my feet as if to say I'm coming home with you, Tom said "Well, that's your answer", "how much do you want for him?" Tom looked at me and the dog, thought for a while. "I tell you what on one condition I won't let you have his pedigree, and any time I want to borrow him to mate with a bitch. You can have him for fifty pounds". I opened the Land Rover door and without a word he jumped in, I counted out the money, have you given him a name yet, "Well, Margaret called him Jason", that's good enough for me, I made a fuss and he responded.

I said "You do much picking up Tom", "if ever you need me give me a bell", we shook hands, I had better call out my other half, "are you ready, if you are we have left our daughter in charge, she will be soon leaving school", Margaret said "you must come and see us again", "We will, and you us".

We got back home, the children were absolutely thrilled with the dog, Roma just accepted him as another dog, but I tried to tell them he was not a pet, one day he will have to work. So his home will be in the kennel, but he will come out quite a bit, his name is Jason.

We had been in touch with Wally and Peg also Nell and Reg. Both were pleased we had settled and would like to come and see us, Colin and Tricia had settled in their school and liked it.

I found a dead tree that needed clearing. It had fell across one of the main rides in the woods, so I set to it and logged it up, loaded it in the trailer and took it up to the big house. The butler came out he was pleased and said "They're some good dry logs", Grandma poked her head out the door "Good morning, Ted", and I blurted out "Good morning, Grandma".

I was thinking about rearing more birds, but how many does he want, and how many days Shooting does he want, I think I will have to get hold of the agent and have a word. Next time I saw them I asked if they knew exactly what the Boss wanted, well, we know he wants more birds and a number of days, I said how about if I suggested day olds and reared them in huts under gas heaters with one large gas bottle to each hut and then sections, so as they get bigger they can go outside with a big net over each one. He said "I know just what you mean, have you met the Keeper at Littleberry?" "Is that the one that borders a bit of the estate where the long gully runs down with a trickle of water runs through?" "Well, all that belongs to us".

I phoned Tom Parry, he asked how the dog was, I said he's great, coming on nicely, "Do you know the Keeper Howes at Littleberry?" "Oh I meant to have told you about him, he's one we call the king, I go picking up sometimes for him, he boarders a bit of your ground, Sid Spademan a grand gentleman have you got a pen handy I will give you his number, you must meet him".

I began to know why they call it the bush telegraph every Keeper knows everybody else, I made a point to go and see the Keeper at Littleberry, he was pleased to see me, had been in the job all his life, so there's not much he didn't know. He showed me the set-up he had for rearing, it was the same as I had in mind, because it was important to both being the same borders we both knew birds will stray across, he was also a very keen clay Shooting man, "Anything I can help you with give, me a shout".

Every time I went home, I had something different to tell her, the agent had orders from the Boss, anything I wanted to improve the Shoot, I should have.

Mr Clark rang, Barbara answered, "Is Ted about?" she said, "I have not seen him since he went out this morning", "When you do see him, ask him to come to the house, we have a big tree we are worried about".

Dinner time came, Barbara told me about the tree they had on their lawn. I went up in the afternoon and found the gardener, we introduced our selves, I'm Ted Rogers and he was Jim Smith, "have you come to look at this tree she keeps on about? It's down on the big lawn" "Let's have a look, walking across the lawn a voice called out coo-ee", Jim said "she's seen us", she came over, "I see you've met, good, well, that's the tree", a magnificent big oak, I could see straight away what the trouble was, she said "We are afraid that big branch is going to break off, from the house it's going to spoil the look of the whole tree, Ted what do you suggest?"

I said "Let's stand back and have a look, Jim how do you feel about making a feature of it so as to leave the branch, I can cut out a big strut, this will mean some help from the farm".

I can show you what I mean standing under the branch, we can bring a tractor in with a front end loader, lift it gently and put a block of concrete in the ground, place a strut under the branch and lower it down or even put two struts in and make it into an archway, plus if you wanted you can grow a clematis up each strut" her face beamed with a smile, "Jim what about that", "what about my lawn", I quickly said "That won't be damaged, can you lay boards down?"

She said "We have had nothing like this done before, I think it's quite exciting, Jim I'm sure you can find the right clematis".

"Tea time", Barbara said "we had a visitor this afternoon, I just let Jason out for a run and someone came riding down the Drive on a bicycle, I made the dogs sit and stay, it was a woman, she said "Hello, I guess you are Mrs Rogers, Trevor's Mum, I'm Mrs Morris Alek's Mum, Trevor told us about his family", they shook hands and had a little chat, "I will let the dogs have a run and then you must come in for a cup of tea", she said "All the time we have been up at Hatch hill Farm I have never been down here."

"Now the dogs have had a bit of exercise, let's go inside, by the way I'm Barbara", "I'm Joan, isn't this a beautiful old building, but what a name The Gas House", they both had a laugh, it's good job we know why it's called that. Well, the boys get on well, together I'm sure Trevor will visit you a lot now your closer".

I cut out two heavy strut posts and left them where they were too heavy to carry, I found the manager and explained what I was asked to do, he helped me out, "Yes of course we can, if I drop a dozen boards off will that be enough, or perhaps it had better be another half dozen tomorrow morning nine o'clock, if you're there I will send three of four men, you have two holes out already to drop the blocks in. The heavy front loader tractor will be available, Ted you must tell them just what you want and where".

I told Barbara what we was doing, she grabbed and gave me a hug, "Please be careful", "I will, you see to Jason for me" I said to Colin and Tricia jump in the front of the

Land Rover, I can drop you off on the way" "Thanks Dad."

I found Jim and between us we worked out just where to make the lift on the branch and dug the holes out for the blocks, I glanced up at the house and saw we had two spectators, Grandma and Mrs Clark. I thought of how my Dad would have tackled this job, he certainly would not have had the tractor available.

The farm lads came, the tractor was measured up to come through the gate after we had put down the boards, "you happy with that Jim?" I asked, I could see he was worried about his precious lawn. I waved the tractor on slowly, I thought if that thing slides off, we will be in real trouble, but slowly done it, I had filled two bags of straw like cushions so the metal would not scrape the bark off the branch, he slowly lifted the branch, I stopped him to hold. Jim was stood well back waiting for something to go wrong, I got two men on each post I had told them exactly what to do, it wasn't easy, but they did it, "Hold on lads for the lower".

I beckoned the Driver to lower, inch by inch, the branch onto the cushions of straw, we got the measurements just right, the posts took the weight perfectly. Now for backing the tractor back up the boards, I need not have worried, it all went perfect to the plan, we all walked down to the tree to have a look at a good job done, and I was pleased.

I heard someone say "Well done everybody", it was the Mrs and the maid with a tray full of tea, and she came to me and patted me on the back, "Thank you Ted very much". She looked at Jim, "What do you think of that Jim?" "I did not think it could be done, but I've already got two clematis to plant". Between us we picked up all the boards and not a mark on the lawn, she came running after me, "Ted have you got a minute, there's another tree I would like you to look at, It's the other side of the garden". It was a tall Beech dying back from the top, "if you look at the base of the tree it's covered in fungus, it will eventually die, do you advise to cut it down", "Well, there's only one way it can go and that's out in the field, I will need a tractor because you can see its leaning back", "Can you keep it in mind Ted, I will have a word with the Boss".

I got home and Barbara wanted to know how it went, "Perfect" I said, "how has your day gone?" "Jason is very good", "Would you like to start him on a whistle?" "Can I"? "Yes of course you can, after tea I will show you". "Oh by the way, Nell rang this afternoon, can they come up for a week, they won't need a room because they have bought themselves a caravan, well you know we will have a lot of fun with them, if you ring them and tell them they can park it in the yard".

"Here's a whistle, I've tried him a couple of times, tell him to sit, go a little way, call him and blow two blasts then stop calling and just blow the whistle. Let's try it, have a small biscuit as a treat when he gets it right, when he gets fed up that's the time to stop, like now".

On one of my walk rounds I saw a number of squirrels and the damage they were doing to some of the trees, I saw the manager and asked him about getting some traps, he said to go to the office and get a ticket. Keep it, whenever you want anything go to Watsons.

So I went in and got two dozen fen tunnel traps and soon got some down making a natural tunnel with some logs and sticks covered over with leaves and soil, put the safety hook on, lifted the plate, pushed the trap to the middle of the tunnel, with a stick pegged it down, lifted the hook off, I had done this many times before but not on this amount. I made sure I would visit each trap every day that was the law, or tried to. I had my eyes set on a bit of a clearing in

the wood quite close to home that would be one place for a release pen. I was in the field by my house one afternoon, a Land Rover came across the track, I could see it was the Boss, he got out and came to me, "Good afternoon, Rogers", I was polite and said "Good afternoon, sir". He said "I must congratulate you on securing the branch on the oak tree on the lawn, Mrs Clark is delighted with it", "Thank you, Sir."
I can see you deep in thought, "Well, I would like to have a piece of this field for a rearing", "Yes the agent told me what your idea is and it is very much the same as most estates, so I think we can go along with that. As for the days, I would like eight guest days and two father and son days, if we say two hundred plus a day, your wanting day-olds we won't cut corners, let's say two and half thousand day-olds, how does that sound?" "Very good to me sir", "Right now, I will leave it completely in your hands to get just what you want."
"Now there's one other thing with the forestry work I want you to do, I would like you to have help, have you got anyone in mind?" "Well, there's a chap on the farm that is interested in my work" "Which one would that be?" "That's John Fox" "Right, I will call in the office if you think he's the chap you would like, I will see if I can poach him for you, and tell him to come and find you", "Thank you very much, sir, I appreciate that."
After he had gone I went to Barbara she said, "That looked a serious talk", "Well, it was, he told me to go ahead and get what I wanted and also said I must have someone to work with me, I am glad about that". That night a knock on the door, I went to the door and there was John Fox, "Hello Ted, I hear you are looking for a mate", "Come in John", we sat down and had a chat over a coffee. "Well, I was surprised when the Boss came to me and said with the amount of work I have got on Keepering and the woods I

got to have some help, your time will be flexible with me, you like a bit of clay Shooting, and I will see you get cartridges for vermin Shooting".
"Well, I would want you to show me how to use a chain saw properly", "You've no need to worry John there will be a good many other thing I will show you, now when do you want to start?" "Next week will do me Ted", "Right, I will see the manager John Cook and he will probably want a word with you" "Does your wife work, John?" Barbara asked, "I would like to meet her" "I'm sure she would like to meet you her name is Susan, we got one boy, he goes to the local school and she works in the local carpet factory in Buckingham".
Barbara had a call from Mrs Clark early one morning, "Barbara, can you do me a big favour, I have to go to London today can you have Jamie for the day, I will drop him off shortly on the way", "Yes, of course I will" she said. She dropped him off hardly without stopping, "I will try not to be too late tonight".

There was one place badly eaten off by rabbits, so I set to busy gassing them, this was with a powder called Cymag, you had to fill in some holes, then put a spoon full in the others and then quickly fill them in, and doing this meant I had to wear a mask and glasses and gloves, it was quite nasty stuff and had to carry it in a sealed container.
John Cook the manager called in home to see me, I always told Barbara where I would be if she wanted me, he knew where I was, he had John with him. He never came close, I put my hand up, he waited until I had finished filling in, then I walked over to them.

"That's some nasty stuff Ted", "it can be if you're not careful!" "Well, I got John with me", "I gather you would like him to work with you, if that's what John wants",

"Yes I would like him with me", "Well, I've had a word with the Boss and we have come to a different pay deal and the hours will be as you want them Ted, is that right John?" "Yes I'm happy with that".

It was nearly nine o'clock in the evening before Mrs Clarke came to pick Jamie up, she was full of apologies, I must get him in his bed, I will come down and have a chat in the week Barbara, thank you again.

As far as my money went, I was quite happy with the bank statements, it was way above whatever I expected. Mrs Clark kept to her word and came to see Barbara, she asked her in for a cup of tea and quite intrigued with where we had been and where we had lived and then said to Barbara, "Have you ever been away for a holiday?" "We haven't, we only had the odd weekend". "Well, I'm going to insist you have a week's holiday" "Well, it will have to be before the end of April because the chicks will be here in May". "Now I want you to take this and tell Ted he must take you away for a holiday, I think he may be asked to have the older boys soon".

"She gave me this envelope, I haven't opened it yet," I said "Why not? She gave it to you, go on open it", she took out a cheque, "Oh my god", she said "it's a cheque for two hundred pounds", "Well, I told you the way they spend money", again I said "it's how the other half live."

That night I phoned Wally and asked him about having a holiday with us in Ireland, I knew he liked a bit of fishing, but this would be fishing of a difference: sea fishing. I told him I been talking to someone who had been to a place called Scibereen, marvellous fishing, I told him that Nell and Reg wanted to come and stay again with us, he said he would look through the holiday brochure,

"Leave it with me, I will fix it with Nell and Reg" I agreed with John to go to the workshop every morning at the wood yard, he could have a key to get in, unless I wanted him to do something else, I showed him how to set the tunnel traps how very soon learned that, I took him up to Hatch Hills there was a god planation of soft wood up there, which in my opinion needed brushing up, I showed him by knocking the lower branches off as high as you could reach with a hook. That was one place I was hoping to put a release pen, I also showed him where a patch of sunflowers will be.

We had a phone call from John and Dorrie saying at last they had got the Keepers job up in Norfolk close to Huntstand, we were getting phone calls from all over from people we had met, wanting to how we were getting on. We had a call from Wally saying he would be in touch with Nell, in a weeks' time as he did when you were at Markgate, and he had found a cottage in Ireland on a farm under the purple mountain, close to the gap of Dunlow. We agreed to meet at the hotel called The Stags Head on the road just outside Holyhead Harbour, Friday night at about eight o'clock to catch the first ferry to Dublin in the morning, he had fixed everything, he was so pleased we were having a holiday together. Barbara was over the moon, he did say he who gets there first waits for the other.

I managed to catch up with Mrs Clark and told her and thanked her for the envelop she gave Barbara. I told John he could start to put the fence up round what will be the rearing field, he could use the Land Rover to get the posts and wire down there.

Pauline was about to leave school, after looking for a job She had the day off, walking Colin and Tricia down the Drive and waited for Nell and Reg to come, I told Pauline we will ring when we got over there, she was getting quite grown up now, she said "Don't worry Mum, I will take them down each morning and get them at home time".

We gave ourselves plenty of time and had two breaks on the way Come the evening we found The Stags Head, Barbara drove coming down, we both dropped off to sleep, suddenly a rattle on the window woke us, Wally had found us, kisses for the girls and a handshake, we were pleased to see one and other. Both the girls had taken sea sickness pills although it was not bad.

We arrived early morning, and well on the road, the further west we went, the more spectacular the mountains and valleys, we knew we were close, there was a sign pointing to the Gap of Dunlow, but did not want that today, we carried on a bit further, found a small farm and directly behind it was this beautiful Purple Mountain, it was simple covered in purple heather. We knew this had to be the place.

A young lad was getting some ponies harnessed, we asked, is this Dunlow Farm, a woman Mrs O'Sulivan came out and asked "Are you Mr and Mrs Rogers?" we both replied "Yes we are here for a week" "Yes welcome to Dunlow. Bring your cars up to the house", it was a small house, she let us in, the table was laid, there's tea and coffee and milk, the rayburn is fuelled by bog blocks, there's a stack of them at the side of the house. "I will leave you a pint of fresh milk each morning".

"Which way is the best to go to Scibereen when you go out from here?" "Turn right and head for Bantry Bay, you will see it sign posted from there, and if you want the Gap of Dunlow you can Drive down, but please be very careful, it's very narrow in places and with rocks either side, very much a tourist attraction, pony and traps constantly up and down."

There was two bedrooms each looked out onto the mountain it was truly a beautiful spot, I said to Wally,

"Let me pay what we owe you for the cottage and ferry",

we agreed to put fifty pounds each in the kitty for electric and food. He insisted we took his car every day. I must admit it was much bigger and better than ours, roof rack, big boot, we both took fishing tackle, he got a bit cross when I offered him money for petrol, I don't think we have ever had a bad word between us before, and we are not going to start now, the girls between them said you had better not, we won't allow it, we laughed and hugged each other and had a strong drink.

The girls had already agreed which room we were having we kissed goodnight and see you in the morning, we were all pretty tired. What I heard in the morning we all had a good night's sleep, we talked over breakfast.

Wally and I said "If we can have one good day's fishing, you girls can have the rest of the week", they decided we go to Lake Killarney first, we had a lovely day there, we had a picnic and a boat trip. Next day we found the Blarney Stone and had a ride round, can we go shopping? They asked. We looked at the map, if you want a big town, Cork will be the best but we will have to be away early because it's quite a way, we all agreed.

When we found it, we thought it was a pretty awful place, mainly because we got lost a couple of times but had some laughs on the way. Finally we found the main shopping area, plenty of gift shops and pubs, we had a good day. We asked the girls if they were happy, 'yes we have had a good time', Wally said "Ted and I would like to go off tomorrow if that's alright. Shall we go fishing if we go early we can have a look at Bantry Bay and follow the coast round to Scibereen it was a good low rocky shore line" We saw a lone chap fishing which gave us incentive to have a go. As usual, we carried all our bits and pieces with us, and we made sure the girls had the chairs and a good spot so they could see us. Ted said "The man that told me back home recommended we use a string of feathers," as a bit of fun we had a small bet who will get the most and suddenly we spotted what looked like the sea was boiling in a huge ring, we called the girls over, what on earth is that, we had never seen anything like it before, it must be fish, like little boys we were quite excited, Peggy said "Well, throw your hook in." Wally was the first in and soon his rod nearly bent double, I stood looking, one wound in and on four hooks out of six we had fish on, the girls were as excited as we were, "They're mackerel! they shouted, what are we going to do with them", Wally had thrown his back in I said "I'll go back and get one of the cool boxes, the ice will keep them".

So I cast my line in and between us we were pulling out fish galore, our arms were beginning to ache. Every now and then it went quiet, as we watched, the shoal of fish going round in a big circle, so we gave up for a while and had a drink and something to eat and a lot of chat.

After a while, we decided to have another go, we took the other ice box, the ice was still solid, we were soon pulling fish in and very soon filled the box and realised we had got enough, so we packed up the gear and went back to the girls. Have you caught enough? we had completely lost the fact we had a bet on, so we called it a draw.

It was getting on towards mid-afternoon, so we all agreed to pack up and take a leisurely trip back to Purple Mountain, we went back more inland and saw much more of the countryside horse's cattle sheep and donkey's running wild, took a lot of photographs, and bog plots being dug out and stacked to dry.

We got back to the farm, Mrs O'Sullivan came out, "have you had a nice day" she asked, "We have had a marvellous day, the fishing was spectacular", we showed her one box, "Good gracious me!" without a word she said "We will take them off your hands," Wally said "we've got some in another box", she said "We will have all you've got", she

called her son over to help, "carry these into the house, Danny".
We carried the boxes in and tipped them onto the big table, she counted them out, its good they're still nice and fresh, Wally was counting as well, "I can't believe that!" he said, "how many Mr Rogers?" he said "One hundred and forty one". Danny had already started gutting them and packing them in the freezer, she said "That's free milk and I'll give you ten pounds towards your electric", we both said a big thank you, and she said "It will help us through the coming winter."
We went up to the house all smiles, and the girls said what are you so happy about, when we told them, "Well, that's what you call a good ending let's have a drink."

We had some food over from the day out, we got the chairs out and sat under the mountain it really was a beautiful sight, we all said how quickly the days were going by, there's one place we haven't been yet, all together we said Gap of Dunlow, we were all a very happy because we don't have to start so early in the morning because we passed the turning just down the road, Ted said "In that case we can have another drink" by the time we had finished we were all ready for bed.
We were told the Gap of Dunlow was a tourist attraction, it wasn't until we got going that we realised what it was all about.
It was a very narrow valley running through the mountains and suddenly a pony and trap appeared, the further we went, more pony and traps seemed to appear, and they made sure they had the right of way. The mountains gradually gave way to a large opening, crowded with people and cars and many more ponies. It was certainly a beautiful place and surprisingly plenty to do, ice cream stalls and just sit back on benches and watch other

people doing silly things and listen to music.
Sadly it was time to talk about coming home, all good things must come to an end, we said our goodbyes to Mr and Mrs O'Sullivan and thanked them for a wonderful holiday. We caught the early morning ferry, we agreed that if we parted we would meet at the same hotel along the road to say our goodbyes. This we did, Wally and I vowed to keep in touch, his last word was, "I still want you to come and work with me one day, my house will become vacant".
It wasn't too late when we got home, the children were pleased to see us, Nell and Reg helped unpack, Nell said "You must have a lot to tell us," the children had their presents. In the morning over breakfast, we asked Nell and Reg if everything was alright, "Yes, Pauline looked after us, in fact we want to ask if we can stay another week?" "Oh Nell, you're an angel, you know you're more than welcome to stop."

John had got the fence round the field and a number of poles to use for perches. A lorry came that week loaded with huts and run sections and heaters. The gas cylinders would come later. John could not believe the stuff we were getting, Reg wanted to help, all the heaters and pipes went down into the shed in the yard.
Barbara shouted "Ted, you're wanted at Darrel House," I told them to wait and have a drink while I was gone. Mrs Clark was waiting for me, "Ted, thank you for coming, can you have John and Tom for the rest of the day? I will take Jamie with me," I said "Well, I got a lorry load of equipment just come," "Well, you know you can deal with them and make them help, Barbara will find them lunch and she knows this", that's why she dropped Barbara an envelope now and then.
"You behave yourselves for Mrs Rogers," with that she

bundled them in the Rover and back home.

We started to lift the sections off, I gave the boys a job to carry the drinkers and small feed troughs down to the shed in the yard, the oldest one said "Ted, we don't want to do that", I said with the men looking on, "Now you listen to me, it's not Ted, it's Mr Rogers to you and don't you forget it, is that clear? I've had a sound message from Mother, if you don't want to help, go and sit under that tree and don't move, we have got work to do".

I had marked out roughly where each hut will be and six pen sections to each hut, the boys came round to doing something by doing as I asked, Barbara brought us all out a cup of tea and the lorry was on its way. John said "When do we start putting them up?" I said "As soon as we can, if you check some of the traps on your way down in the morning, I will come straight out and start putting one or two together." I took the boys home and Grandma kept her eye on them, but I always thought they would be up to some sort of mischief, they were always plaguing Grandma with tricks, but she never held back on using her walking stick when she got the chance. I was always glad to know when they were going back to boarding school.

While we were putting the hut together, John asked me if I knew the estate had a cricket team and would I join, I said "Of course and Colin was old enough to play", "Well, someone will soon be mowing it", it was up the main Drive to the old estate home, Tile House, which was all paid for by the estate, and Barbara was included with the other women to do the teas.

We were putting the last hut together, I could see it was the Bosses' Land Rover coming across the field and they all jumped out, him and her and the four kids, three boys and the little daughter I had not met before. "Well, Rogers this looks very impressive", "Twelve huts, two thousand five hundred day olds," she said "Ted, tell me how this is going to work," I naturally said "Yes Madam I can". I showed them both how it will work, the gas bottles outside each hut and heaters inside. But when the time comes to let them out, won't they fly over, no because there will be a net over each pen. "Well boys, don't you think this year will be exciting? This year will be the first year we have had a proper organised Shooting season," I looked at the boys and said, "I can assure you it will be properly organised."

"This is something else, I want you to give Tom as much time as you can in handling of guns, John is not so keen, they both have twelve bore shot guns and I would like you to keep them at your house, where there is a lockup case fastened to the wall and you won't forget the tree we looked at, at Dayrell House?" "No I haven't forgot but we must have this lot up and ready for the seventeenth of May when the chicks will arrive."

"Is everything all right for you John?" "Yes thank you sir," Madam said "I must go down to see Mrs Rogers while I'm down here, Jacqueline you come with me."

Barbara saw her coming down the field so went to meet her, they both greeted each other, "Barbara this is Jacqueline," "Hello Jacqueline," "Say hello to Mrs Rogers, Barbara may I ask you to have her also from time to time", "Yes of course," "Thank you very much, Barbara we must go and catch the others."

I said to John not another word about how much it's costing, how the other half live and we are nowhere near finished, we want at least two release pens, one up at Hatch Hills and one in the home wood.

John asked about that big beech tree that is laying back over the garden, "That will test us, you can drive that big tractor from the farm, it's got to go through a narrow gap into the field and then it's got to be cut up and stacked to dry out and then we will have to start the release pens".

I have had a word with the agents and they agreed for us to thin some larch trees: out, so we will be alright for posts, when we do that we can bring some poles back to the yard and saw out some stakes if we get any wet weather.

We will try and do that tree this week, I will see John Cook about the tractor and see if they've got a wire rope, I told John I'd like to borrow the big tractor and did he have a wire rope and was there any cattle in the field, because we will have to take the fence down. "Well, I'll come and help take the fence down I want to see you fell this tree" "Well, in that case you can help John with the wire rope, I will put the ladder up so far and climb up to where I want the wire rope round the tree, I will tie a rope onto the hook, I can pull the wire up with you pushing it to me". I got the dee link round onto the wire, I came back down with a fair bit of sweat running , just then, the maid came out with a tray of drinks, "Madam told me to keep an eye out for you", we all thanked Flossy for the drinks.

"Right John, let's have a look at this tree, now I'm going to do the same as my Dad used to do" I stood in front of the tree and looked straight through the gap and then up to the top of the tree, walked out into the field and put a stick in where I reckon the tips will be. The saw was filled, "Now John, come and stand with me at the bottom of the tree, I'm going to cut the sink out and that's not quite a quarter of the way in, now when I cut through I've got to judge just how far to go."

Now, John when I give you the signal, I just want you to take up the slack and when I signal again, you keep going and don't stop until she's on the ground." John took up the slack and held perfectly, I set the saw into the back, once I started I dare not stop, I was about to give John the signal, there was a flash across in front of the tree under the wire, it was too late, John had already taken my signal,

I dare not stop: the tree was already falling. John done exactly what I told him, we stopped when the tree was on the ground.

John Cook ran after the boy, I sat on the tree thinking what could have happened; John brought him back, I was bloody angry, I whipped my belt off an gave him a wallop, I shouted at John Cook, "Take the little sod back to the house".

John Fox came and sat with me, "Hell that was close Ted, but look where the tree fell, smack bang in the middle of the gap", I said "Bugger the tree, that kid could have been killed," Just then Madam came to us, "Ted, John has just told me what happened, I've brought you both out a tot of whisky, Ted I'm deeply sorry this happened, I understand you gave him a whack" "Yes I did madam" "Well, you should have given him more, if you feel you want to go home please do, I will leave the tray on the tree for the glasses".

"John, you want a bit more use of the saw? We will have another hour and then pack up, just knock some of the small stuff off, I'll pull it out of your way and stack it up. Cut the bigger bits into about four foot lengths and I'll stack them up against the hedge." John was not doing bad being he had not used a saw that much, I put him right once or twice, but I could see we were working together alright. I waved to John that was it for the day, we rolled the rope up and John took the tractor back, I asked him to check some of the traps on his way down to me in the morning.

I had the saws sharpened and ready to go, I told Barbara what happened last night, and again before I left the house, she gave me a big hug, "Please be careful, I will see you Dinner time." John was early so we had a good start. John asked how you were going to deal with the tree itself, Meet me at the yard after dinner there are some old pieces of telegraph poles we can use as rollers, I had a small wire rope of my own. So as not to tear up the garden, we levered up the end and slid two pieces of rollers under, I hoped the Land Rover was going to grip , no problems I let John Drive so I knew just how to put the rollers ahead of one another slowly out into the field, left the roller under the tree. Jim the gardener came to see how we were getting on, I asked him if any of the brush wood would be any god to him, "Yes I can make use of that on the flower borders".

I had taken Tom walking with his gun the odd shot at a pigeon, but I felt he had to get a bit of real shooting, but up to now it was mostly the safety side, getting over stiles and through gates, just having one cartridge at a time. I had just discussed this with his mother and she said "the Boss will be delighted" So when he's home from school can you let me know? I will try and find some pigeon decoying. I have their guns and I will pick them up at Dayrell house, "yes I will Ted". I told John what I wanted to do with Tom. And when I take him out I would like you to come and bring your gun" he was pleased to hear that.

I spotted some birds dropping down on some early barley, we quickly pulled some bushes down in the hedge, I made Tom stand back and watch. John and I got two or three down, set them up again , John took a back seat Tom was eager to have a go. I was pleased to see how he handled the gun, he had taken notice of what I had been telling him.

We went back to my house "We've got one job to do before I take you home" I went in the house and brought out the cleaning kit, this is also an important part of Shooting, I put the rods together and made sure he did it properly, John cleaned mine and his, I took Toms gun which was a beautiful twenty bore, I broke it and handed it to him to put in its sleeve, "Now, have you any cartridges in your pockets? No he said, I said "I'm going to ask you one more time", he pulled out two cartridges, "What the hell do you want to take them home for when your guns are here with me? We were about to give you ten out of ten, but you have blotted your copy book! Now get in the Land Rover and wait for me".

"John, let's go in and have a cup of tea" Barbara said "I was watching you, I knew you were not happy with him, he won't do that again." John will you slip through the back and have a look at sluice gates on your walk home? I don't think it's been turned for a long time, if the lakes ever overflow we will be in trouble, I will see you down there Monday morning, check the traps on your way down please."

The huts had to be floored with fine pea gravel so we had to get inside each hut and cut the grass short, plus putting up the release pens. The one at Hatch Hills won't be bad because we make use of the standing larch trees. We got to cut out pegs to hold the strands of electric fence wire run off a twelve Volt battery, and find some long posts for the pen in the home wood.

"John, if we take the trailer can get what we want on that, if we finish the huts today I will meet you in the yard in the morning seven thirty, we can cut out a few pegs and then go down to Watsons as soon as they're open."

John looked at me, "did you know how much of this stuff you want and how much it's going to cost?" "I should do I've been doing it for a while now. All we got to do John is make sure we rear as many birds as we can, to give the Boss some good day's Shooting, what we have got to aim for is the seventeenth of May when the chicks come." I marked the posts out for the wire to be fixed to and a shallow trench for about six inches of wire to be turned out at the bottom and soil to be put back on, and funnels every so far round with guide to run the birds back in they

fly out; and a door so we can get in and out.
John could not believe the trouble I was going to, I told him, you will see one day, well, it looks very impressive. Any dead larch we can pull over and make perches the sooner you can get them off the ground the better, we can put the electric fence round later.
Now we can start on the home wood pen, that won't be quite so easy, I thought I ought to show Tom Good the new set up, I could call in on his bungalow and ask him if he would like to have a look round, "Yes, I would I never had the luxury of a Land Rover," "Well, jump in Tom," I took him first to the rearing field, "what's all this?" he said, "I'll show you Tom, we got twelve huts and they will hold about two hundred and fifty chicks each," "Where are you going to put this lot?" "Well, we will have two release pens, I will take you up to Hatch Hills and show you the ones up there."
"How are you going to Shoot them in there" "We won't Tom, Jump in and I can show you the idea," I drove back out past the farm and stopped, "Now Tom, you see that strip of bear ground? That will be a strip of pheasant cover, we will feed the birds out into that."
"There will be eight guns and eight pegs each will draw a peg, I will take the Beaters right round the bottom of the strip and Drive it back to the wood and then feed them in the pen again until we want to do that Drive again." It was a good job we had a number of sheds, one was for food and one was for the Beaters. The Boss will take his guests back to Dayrell house for lunch, Barbara will do her bit in having jugs of soup to go with their own dinners for the Beaters.
 John asked me "When do we turn the heaters on?" "I think we had better turn them on tomorrow morning that will give the huts time to warm up, if you check the traps on your way down and leave them un-set for a while." We

had two days before the chicks arrived, so we pushed on with the Home wood pen and got the wire up. I was pleased with that, there was only a bit of tidying up to do. Although the children had seen it all before with Barbara, they were quite excited, I had set the heater to the right temperature and just opened the shutters on the windows a wee bit. We set them all up with Feeders and drinkers in each hut.

Two men with van, John, me and Barbara, it did not take long to carry them to each hut in their boxes and we emptied each box, it was good to see them go straight to the heater and peck at the food and drinkers and now it was a twenty four hour watch for a couple of weeks. Feather pecking can develop into cannibalism, you either put specs on the beak or de-beak them by using a hot iron by taking the tip off the top bill. This is a very time-consuming job and then give them a little bit of a run outside to stop the boredom, then all the nets have to go on manly at this stage to stop any attack from overhead birds from taking the chicks quite easily, if not stopped by Shooting or by cage trapping.

What was day old chicks needed the full run of the pen and grew up into fully feathered poults, twelve to fourteen weeks they are ready to go to the wood, this was an early morning job to give the birds' time to settle down and acclimatise to their new surroundings.

Each Keeper has his own way of calling the birds to feed with a whistle from day-olds, there was always a grey area when it came to hunting, some hunters thought they had the right to hunt anywhere, but they did not, they hunt by invitation only. Some Keepers to get rid of the hunt quickly, they would catch and bag up the fox the night before at the furthest point away, loose it out in the morning where ever the hunt met, he was there willing to tell them where they most likely to find one.

I was opposed to this and made it quite clear to the Boss and the master of the hunt, the only time they came was early spring for cub hunting, although I thought a hunt with hounds in full cry was a pretty sight that was it, not on my patch, but the Boss did tell me he would invite them to meet at the house but not to hunt.

We had cleared a wide ride down the middle of Hatch Hills pen and what a sight that was, John came with me each time we fed three times a day to start with we used the same kind of whistle. We needed a trailer for the Beaters and a Game cart because birds had to be hung up as soon as collected, this was sorted by the mechanic, there was a freezer van came round to collect all kinds of Game.

I took the Boss round two days before and showed him where each Drive will be and where the pegs were, although he had been on other Shoots, this was the first time he would be the host and show off his own Shoot. John and I went off early and fed all round, then he waited in the yard for the Beaters to come on two tractors and trailers, he knew just where I wanted him to go, "I will catch up with you later."

I went up to the house, the Boss called them together, I could see he was enjoying this, "Gentlemen I would like you to meet my Keeper, will you take your peg as usual to each Drive! I must warn you the Drive might be a bit hectic," I immediately crossed my fingers, I was glad to see three pickers up, John and Tom had taken it between then to bring a third one. I had agreed with the Boss when they were ready he would blow his whistle, I was pleased to see John had kept the Beaters well back to start with and quiet.

John was at the other end of the line, he put his thumb up, what I did not tell the Boss or John, after I fed this morning I ran a Selwyn line along the end of the cover, this was

one way of making the birds rise up and over the guns.
Suddenly the whistle went and an enormous volley of shots being fired, knowing full well a lot of the men Shooting were experienced and had Shoots of their own, I held the line up for a few minutes I could see there was still a lot of birds in front of us. We moved off and a constant flight of birds going out, I knew that every gun had more than their fair share of birds down, we finally pulled out I blew my whistle that was the Drive, the guns were immediately put in their sleeves and the chatting between them I could see was exciting.

I waved John on to take the Beaters on when they were loaded up and wait for me at the next Drive, I went out to the pickers up and they had a good job, they had let the guns who had dogs, pick close to them which was the right thing to do, they were in a right huddle the hip flasks were going round to each other.

I heard a voice, "Rogers," that could be the Boss, "what a fantastic sight," I didn't know he had brought his wife, "Ted, that was absolutely fabulous," she patted me on the back, she said "I hope they haven't killed too many," I said "You needn't worry about that, madam, I can control that," the other ladies put their hands up and gave me a wave, the Boss whispered to me, "Leave the Land Rovers on the lane and walk across the field, that's right."

Two more Drives before lunch, this one won't be so good but I know they will all get some Shooting and some of these birds will be wild. It was a long winding spinney and pretty rough in places and needed the dogs to work here, the whistle went and the birds went out in a steady trickle and more than I thought in the bag, these will add to it, that Drive over: no pat on the back this time, but I knew by the smiles and laughter between them.

Last Drive before lunch, John had already taken the Beater's away down the field to walk up some of the hedge rows back up to a pond, but they stopped well back and quiet, I had warned the Boss that this Drive could provide a few duck which was well covered with trees and rhododendron's and a small wood to finish with. The whistle went and we were on the way, soon there was some Shooting on the outside, I thought that could only be some duck had gone early.

The Drive over and lunch time, I got the bag for the morning two hundred and seventy five pheasants, fifteen ducks and four woodcock, it was twelve o'clock when they left for Dayrell House. I agreed with the Boss he will be on his pegs for one forty five, I knew he would not be late. The Beaters had well settled for lunch back at Keepers Cottage, Barbara was ready with her favourite Game Keeper's soup, this she brought out in a big old fashioned saucepan, it was ladled into mugs and flask cups and went down very well.

The first Drive was up in the park, a piece of waste ground backed on to Stow Riden scurried over sown with pheasant cover , this drew the birds out from the home wood pen, this kind of idea proved very affective for the birds to fly back home, good high testing birds.

Last Drive of the day was something rarely done, I had released some birds in a pen at the back of Keepers Cottage, the Drive was a long narrow spinney, way out across the field, this meant the guns walked up from the Keeper's house up the field to two rows of pegs four guns in front four guns behind, in the cabbage they were at least forty to fifty yards apart. I was quite happy knowing these men used this idea on their own Shoots, it was very testing for some and an exciting Drive to end the day.

Tom, knowing at the end of the day I would want a brace of birds to take up to Dayrell House and the four woodcock, the Boss came to me, "Rogers, will you come up to the house in just under an hour's time?" "I will Sir thank you," I had already given the Beaters their money at lunch time so they got away when finished.

They all thanked Barbara and said goodbye, I took the Land Rover and parked by the front door and waited for them to come out and in the old fashioned way, took their brace of birds in one hand and cleverly shook my hand with the other with a tip enclosed and expressed their pleasure for a wonderful day, and the ladies also thanked me especially when I told them the bag was four hundred and ten pheasants fifteen ducks and four woodcock. Madam came to me, "Ted, will you come into the house?" I followed her in, the Boss was waiting, he grabbed my hand, "I never expected a tip from him in that way," I felt he had pushed it in my hand, she always did seem affectionate.

"Ted, we have had a most wonderful day thank you again," she showed me to the door, I drove home and realised I still had whatever the Boss gave me was still in my hand. Barbara flung her arms round me, she knew the day went better than expected, I opened my hand and she said "What's that?" I unfolded it and what a shock, a fifty pound note, I said "But that's not all," I pulled my money out of my pocket and reckoned it up. In all it was two hundred and ninety pounds, and it was my turn to give her a hug because she had organised for the birds to be hung up in the cold room, which had been made out of some small sheds at the back of the house, she remembered to switch it on the morning and she had seen to Jason our dog for me.

I had not taken him out today because he was not ready for a big day, Colin was also helpful in many small ways, I'm afraid there's a lot of Shoots do not realise how important a Keepers family is.

Next morning down to earth and I was up early and fed up

at Hatch Hills and quite surprised to see how many birds turned up to feed, a lot were outside the pen so had to be gently walked round to the funnels and back in the pen.
On my way back home I went round the wood yard and met John going home, he had just fed the Home Wood pen, "John I would like you to have this for your help yesterday," "Thank you very much, are you playing this afternoon, I see someone's got the pitch ready, but I will feed round if you are playing." We are going to have to start feeding a bit further out, I see if can find some

forty gallon oil drums and place round about where we need to feed, we will start taking the nets off next week and the sections and stack them in one of the other sheds, we will have to get rid of some of these foxes. I will show you how to set a fox snare, but this will be between us but they will have to be checked every day because they won't always be dead.

I had a visit from the local PC, he was sorry I had not been asked to do too much duty since I had been there. In the Buckingham Force it was much behind as far as the social side, there was no social involvement Club compared to the Gloster Force were, there was a lot of sport such as tug-of-war competitions, he agreed that side of life was falling to one side, but said he would keep more in touch. In fact he would like my Shoot dates, and I asked him to come as a Beater. He might be surprised how much information he would get from the countryside. He was pleased to hear this, we shook hands he said, "I will pass this on to the inspector," which he did, and gave me and the Boss a visit and said the estate office would be a focus point to be reporting from, in future."

The freezer van came to pick up the Game, he said he would take rabbits and deer, I had to put this point to the agent and the Boss and the damage the Mont Jack deer were doing to the forestry and to the crops in the fields, they agreed there was too many on and running through the estate and they had to be controlled, they told me to do this and dispose of them as I see fit, I applied for a rifle licence and got it, this was the most efficient way of killing deer and rabbits.

Pauline had left school and was working, Colin and Tricia were growing up fast, and the years were rolling by. Nell and Reg had paid a visit on their way to Scotland for a holiday, Wally and Peggy had come and spent some time with us and enjoyed every minute, he liked a bit of rabbit shooting. A month ago he told me Dad wasn't very well, and that was one reason they came up to tell me he had passed away. He had always said, he did not want any fuss, so that's the way we kept it, I said that's okay Wally, we sat on the garden seat and talked quietly, him and I were always very close. I asked how long he had off, I've got the rest of the week, why not stop with us for the rest of the week, I am sure Peg would like to, let's go in and have a drink and ask her. "Oh, I would love to."

We went out and about, I left John to do what he thought if I was not about, they were on their way home the end of the week, his last words, "Don't forget, as soon as my house is free, I want you to come and work with me," one day I will.

As one Shoot season finished, getting ready for the next, when suddenly the dreaded foot and mouth disease broke out. All estates and farms were closed down, as luck had it, we had not ordered any chicks, so I had a job putting 'Keep Out' signs blocking off footpaths, John went back onto the farm for a couple of days a week.

All main gateways were dug out and made into big baths filled with water and disinfectant, and a bucket and brush by every garden gate and a matt of straw.

It was very rarely I went shopping with Barbara, but this day she wanted me to go with her and we had a coffee and done a bit of shopping, she said "Let's have a look in here," in she went, I said "I don't know what you want to look at baby clothes for," She looked at me and smiled, that told me one thing, I said "You're not," "Yes I am" and gave a girlish giggle.

We got to school and waited for Tricia and Colin to come out, I said are we going to tell the children, well, let's wait till after tea, and we will have a guessing Game first and then tell them. I asked if she knew when, well, it could be early November, I have got to make an appointment next week to see the doctor, well, that's something you can do tomorrow morning. Look through that old holiday brochure and see if you can find a cottage to rent, if not I will phone Uncle Wally and Aunty Peg I know they would be pleased to have us for a week, thought it might be too late to find a holiday cottage. I phoned Wally and said we would like to take a break when the children were on their school holiday, any chance of coming down, he jumped at the idea, yes of course you can, so that was something we could look forward to.

Barbara's visit to the doctor confirmed she was expecting and it would be the beginning of November, I was pleased about that, she won't have the Shoot to worry about and I will be able to spend more time with her. We had our holiday with Wally and Peg and a good time was had by all and was so pleased to hear the news, we had to tell them.

One day she wasn't feeling too well, I called the doctor, he said he would like her to go into Alsbury Hospital for a check-up and she wasn't too happy when they said they would like her to stay for a rest until the baby was born, two weeks later she had a baby boy and all went according to plan.

I went in to see her, Sister said can you take her home tomorrow, I brought them home and next day tried to impress on Barbara to take things easy for a while but knowing how she was always on the go I didn't get very far. Pauline came home from work, joined hands with Tricia and holding baby's hands said together, Oh not another brother and gave him a kiss.

I did take Tom out on the odd walk with a gun, I did let him shoot a cock bird for the big house, one action, he dropped the bird across the river and I never had the dog with me that day, I said I will come back later and pick it up. He wasn't satisfied with that. A bit further on there was a two-strand fence across the river, I knew what he was about to do, I took the gun off him, he stood on the bottom strand and held onto the top, got half way across and started to wobble and in he went, the river wasn't deep so I shouted to him to get up walk out. "What's Mummy going to say?" I said "She will probably bring you back and chuck you back in, you have got to learn to listen, get in the Land Rover."

I got him back home Mummy was not very pleased. I explained what happened, she just laughed and said "next time you do that, I will have a camera ready. Thank you Ted, will you come and pick Lucy up in the morning? I meant to have rung Barbara about nine thirty please." I wondered what she will say when she hears our news, "I don't want her to know yet" Barbara said "I want her to keep giving me that little brown envelope" But of course we never reckoned on Lucy going back and telling her Mummy she had seen a baby at Mrs Roger's house.

I had taken Lucy back home about four thirty, the phone rang, "Barbara it's Mrs Clark, I do apologise for sending Lucy down. If I knew you had visitors, I certainly would not have done so." Barbara quickly stopped her, "Madam, I'm glad to say our visitor will be a long term one, would you please find time to come down and see me," "well, I'm home tomorrow, the boys have gone to London, do you mind if I bring Lucy?" "Oh please do," "I will see you about ten o'clock."

I made sure I was going to be close by, I had Jason in the field doing a bit of training, I had about finished when she arrived and stood watching for a while. I put the dog in his kennel and said good morning, we walked to the house, and Barbara was ready to greet her "Good morning Madam come in and let me introduce you to our latest addition to the family," she picked him up, "This is

Martyn Rogers," Madam stood open mouthed, being a mother, "Can I hold him? I must sit down Barbara, how, when, why didn't you let me know," "Because we didn't want any fuss," "But you must have a little help, please let me help, you must have some rest, with your permission I will send someone I know to come and help you either in the home or to help with the children, I must add this will not cost you any expense because on the odd occasion I will ask you to have Lucy for the day when I go out to business, one other thing, can you give me your doctor's phone number? I will see he gives you a regular visit and a personal consultation until you feel you no longer need it." "Right, Lucy, we have got to say goodbye to this lovely baby, but we will keep in touch, Ted, you will promise me if there's anything you want you will let me know," "thank you Madam I will" she patted me on the back and said goodbye and in the car and away.

I went back in the house Barbara said "Look what she left, another brown envelope," and I said, "How the other half live, we have never had so much money before, but on the other hand they have never been able to off-load the boys and the girl on anybody before," I said, "if you don't want all this fuss, what do you think she asked." I said "if I could afford it that's what you would have, but it's not costing us anything so why not accept it."
A knock on the door, I was in the shed at eight o'clock the next morning, I never heard the car pull up in the yard, I heard Roma give one bark in the house, I looked out there was a young lady stood there nicely dressed, I asked "Can I help?" "Mr and Mrs Rogers?" yes, "I am Sally Rose, a home help, Mrs Marsh contacted me and to help in any way I can." I said, "Well, she never gave your name do you mind if I ring her!" I rang and Grandma answered, I said who I was, "Hello, Ted I'm afraid Madam is not here,

can I help you." "I have a lady here she tells me Madam has sent her to us," is that Sally Rose, "yes Grandma, that's all I wanted to know," I apologised to the lady and said I was sorry, "You were quite right to be cautious, please call me Sally," come in and meet Barbara, Roma looked on curiously, "Is your dog safe?" I said "He will do just what I tell him, he thinks the world of Barbara and the children, if you take your coat off I will take it and hang it up."

Barbara had just come in the room, Roma immediately went to her and she made a fuss of him, "If I give you the baby, you sit down and call him to you and talk to him I will sit by you and talk to him and make a fuss, he will smell you and smell the baby and me." "I must say I have never been introduced to a family and a dog," Ted said "I can promise you he will accept you as one of the family, you must never show any dog you're afraid of them." "Well, Roma are you going to let me have a look round." "Barbara, how do you feel about having some home help, I promise you it's nothing to be ashamed of, I'm not only home help, I'm also a state registered nurse and if they are willing to help you, they must have a lot of faith in you and appreciate the work you do for them, so my advice to you is to accept it.

 Now where would you like me to start, shall I put him in his carry cot? I can see you have bathed him, he is a very healthy little baby, can I make a suggestion, would you like me to make a cup of tea? Ted, may I call you Ted," Well why not, "I do not know how long I will be coming, my orders are to visit as long as needed, shall we sit down and have a chat, I would like to know about the family," Ted asked "Can I leave you for an hour I've just got some birds to feed up the Home Wood, "You won't be long will you," "No if I bump into John I will get him to do it." I did see John so I was back early, I took a bucket of coke in for the Rayburn, this heated the house as well, as the water, Sally said "You are very cosy in here, Ted I've heard a lot about your lovely family, you have moved around a bit," "Yes but that's the nature of the job, maybe this one we will settle here, my Dad always said you never know what's round the corner."

I had just got back from feeding, went in to the house for a drink, a car pulled up in the yard, Barbara looked out the window, it's the doctor, I went to the door, "Dr Hayes, it's Mr Rogers. I've had a call to see your wife may I come in?" Yes of course, "Hello Mrs Rogers, Mrs Clark has asked me to call and make sure you are keeping well, this little fellow is doing okay, I must say your dog is very well, behaved," he will do what I tell him.

Barbara not being used to all this fuss and attention, was beginning to get a bit unsettled, I could see this happening so I gently spoke to her one day, to give it a couple of more days and at the end of the week I will put a stop to it. I had a quiet word with Sally and said I thought Barbara was perfectly well enough to carry on with our normal way of life, and I will not require her service any longer but thanked her very much for her help and promised I would call her if needed, the Doctor also said he will call in a months' time. Immediately I could see a happier Barbara, she said how people could just sit back and do nothing, and be waited on hand and foot, it's not for me, I gave her a cuddle and said well, that's how the other half live, but it's not for us.

I did thank Madam for her help and concern for Barbara, "Tell her I will call round to see her shortly, and ask if she could have Lucy for two days next week!" Her response to me was, "I certainly won't have a guilty conscience in taking that brown envelope now!" She came down and dropped Lucy off as normal and if Ted would bring her back six o'clock tonight and here's the brown envelope, she kept it and opened it in front of me, "Wow," she said "A hundred pounds, that's fifty a day she's been giving me," Ted said, "Well, I wonder how much she's making at all these business meetings? We will have another holiday soon" she said, "I think we deserve one".

I had taken the two boys out with their guns a few times, Tom was beginning to realise the do's and don'ts at least that's while he was with me. It was one day the boys were left with Grandma, I was in the wood at the back of the house when Barbara called me and told Roma to speak with two of his barks, I knew I was wanted, I ran back to the house, it's grandma on the phone, "Hello Ted, come quickly the little devils have blown the house up! I was in the Land Rover like a shot.

When I arrived the butler was at the door, "They're going to kill us one day," I ran in, made sure I found Grandma, she was in the kitchen having a coffee at the time in the lounge, "Ted, it wasn't so bad as it looked, the butler had cleaned it up after opening the windows and letting the smoke out" It was a good job it was a big old fashioned chimney and with very few hot ashes in, but enough to make a mess.

I ran out and grabbed Tom and John, dragged them back in, Grandma was not backwards in giving them a wallop with her walking stick I eventually learned it was John who had thrown a firework in the fire. The butler and Flossy the maid gave them a cloth to wipe it up, and between us when we had finished, it was back to normal, but Grandma had not finished with the boys, I left the house and left her to it,

Madam came to me one day, "I would like the estate to do something special this year for Christmas, can you come up with an idea." "Yes I'm sure I can!" I mentioned it to Barbara straight away she said "How about an old fashioned pig roast and a real barn dance and make a charge proceeds to charity of their choice?

I wrote it all down, when I saw her I asked what she thought of the idea, this will mean I will have to build a big fire to produce enough red hot coals to stand a spit over. I heard of two butcher brothers who did this sort of thing, they offered to do it on the cheap.

I saw John Cook asked him if it was possible to completely empty one of the big corn barns, this was done and in good time, I asked Madam and the Boss to come and have a look and give their approval, he ordered John to get the butchers to come and pick out the best pig and have it ready.

John Cox helped me build the fire and his wife Susan helped Barbara serve the food out with the help from others, the butchers done the carving, we found an old wagon which we dragged into the barn to make a stage and many bales of straw for seats. Music was provided by a small group from Buckingham who played Country and Western. These were hired by Madam, and tickets were sold none stop.

A surprise visit one day from Sally Rose who was the home help, madam had asked her to see Barbara and ask if she could help by looking after Martyn for the day so that she can enjoy herself in the evening, Pauline came with Colin and Tricia. I could see madam and the Boss were having a good time, the bar was doing very well, organised by the pub from Whittlebury. Before the end, came Madam came and patted me on the back and said they had had a wonderful evening, she handed over two hundred and fifty pounds which she gave to the local head teacher who also enjoyed herself. A good time was had by all.

The next day a good gathering of hands was pulled together to tidy up and put back to normal, a great job done by everyone.

Although the estate had been closed down by the disease Foot and Mouth, with Christmas over a few restrictions had been lifted, by April/May the next Shoot was being organised, this pleased Madam and the Boss very much, I was told to carry on as normal.

Barbara and I had decided to have a holiday and had booked a cottage in Scotland in good time, John was keen to look after Jason our dog but had him back home in a kennel.

He carried on putting the last touches to the pens and we would be back the first week in May, well in time for the arrival of the chicks.

We had permission to have the children off school for the holiday. A very nice cottage with plenty of walks and Games, Pauline and Tricia took it in turns to feed Martyn, Colin was always kicking a football around, Barbara had plenty of books to read, we arrived home well rested.

To my surprise while we were away, the manager had taken on a young lad Michael White with a wife and little boy, I did not know who he was or why they had taken him on, but I was asked by the manager if I could find him something to do.

But it wasn't easy with a lad who did not want to work or do anything. Suddenly a series of punctures started to happen, combine tyre let down, the tractor tyre let down, the Land Rover suffered, The police had a look and could not fathom it out, I had a look at some of them, and was sure of a little hole I found had a ring round the outside, The police thought it might be made by a .22 rifle, I said I would like to hold a rifle against the tyre and fire it.

It was a wet day in the yard, in the workshop John and I were sawing out stakes when Michael walked in. He said

"Hello" I asked him if he wanted something to do, he said "Can I use that saw," I quickly switched it off, I don't know why but I felt a little uneasy, I looked at John and winked my eye, "I tell you what you can do, help John wire brush these pieces of iron off ready for welding together"

I was fitting a handle into an axe when I wondered what he was doing, he had picked up a small hand drill. I was making some boxes and was showing John and Michael how we used rubber tyres for latches and hinges, I had cut some strips of rubber.

Michael put the drill to a piece and pushed it right through! I could not believe what I saw. "Well, lads, it's time we packed up and went home for tea, if it's wet I will see you in the shed in the morning" I whispered to John, "Just mess about in the shed until I get there."

I went straight to the office, I could not have been luckier. Two police officers were in reporting for duty, I explained what I had seen, "We can pick him up now" I said "No, you don't, you come in the morning at seven thirty you can catch him red handed in the shed, his name is Michael" It worked perfectly, we were in the shed when two men walked in, "Good morning sir can I interest you in some special boxes we are making, these are my mates John and this is Michael, if you like, Michael can show you how we use a piece of tyre for the hinges" He put the hand drill and wound it right in, bingo.

I realised they were detectives the minute they walked in the door, "Michael you are responsible for all the tyres that have been let down," I could see the lad was ill, he put his hand on his shoulder, "I would like you to come with us Michael," they put the handcuffs on and took him out to the car, John and I sat down, "How the hell did you spot that" "Well, look for yourself, if he had not pushed the drill right in, it was the chuck that made the outer ring"

I had a visit that evening from the police for a statement, they confirmed that he was ill and was in hospital, I asked about his wife, they said that when they came they left a WPC with her and her son and they had now been taken back to Manchester where they came from.

While he was here, he asked if I would do a duty at the Point to Point on Saturday, "Yes I can, it's only for the afternoon," Barbara made sure I looked smart, she was quite proud of me in my uniform she asked did I have some money, yes I've got a pound on me for a drink.
Just walking my little patch I realised it was Grand National day. I stopped at a posh car that had a tele in the boot, the horses were being mounted in the ring and being led out and one that stood out in my mind was Fionavan, an outsider at a hundred to one, I thought I'll find someone to put my pound on, just then the Sargent came round, "Were having a whip round, Ted, a pound each, all going on the favourite" he went on and on and in the end I nearly threw it at him, he went away, "I'll be back with your winnings."
I stood watching the race, the further they went the more fell, I could not believe it, they nearly all fell and one continued, Fionavon went on to win. Before I finished I found the Sargent and said you can keep my winnings and you can have your uniform back I'm resigning from the force from the minute, I returned my uniform to the station and finished, it wasn't the same as before.

This will be our fifth season, John was helping to take more responsibility for the Shoots and his own section of the estate to Keeper, he had his holidays when he wanted them, which pleased him and his wife. The seventh season coming up, the boys were asking for more Shooting, but I still had to keep a strict eye on the cartridges and guns.

Wally had rung me again saying he was at last moving house and was not in a hurry to let anyone in unless it was me.

When the Shoot season was over, one morning when I came down the stairs, Roma never came to meet me, I went to his bed and sadly he had died in his sleep. How was I going to tell Barbara! I waited and pulled myself together and took her a cup of tea up and sat on the bed, she immediately said what's the matter, I had to break the news, she was so upset, we dried our eyes and said "We have to tell the children" Pauline did not want to go to work, Tricia and Colin did not want to go to school, Tricia said "Can we say goodbye to him?" I said I think he would like you to go to school, Mum said "Let's have our breakfast and then we'll say goodbye together and then Dad will take you down to school and fetch you home," Pauline did not go to work.

I came home and phoned Wally, I asked him if we could come down for a few days, they were very pleased to hear that we will come down at the beginning of the Easter holidays, the huts and pens were all ready for the chicks, although it was a couple of months to go before they came.

The house the Boss lived in before they came to Dayrell, a little way down the road, which they kept on but rented out. In the grounds they had built what they called a play house for the four children, it was a full size bungalow but no inside interior. The Boss told me he had ordered a firm from London to come and build a full size scalectric set which went right round the inside of the building, would I keep an eye on it. I didn't know the boys were home. I went down there one day, I found their bikes thrown down in the Drive-way. I quietly walked up and they were having a whale of a time with the trains going round, cars as well, it must have cost a fortune and sat in the middle of the room the three boys and a little girl. The oldest had air rifles shooting at the track, I was so angry to think they had so much, I simply walked away, I did not want to know how the other half lived.

I went back home and told Barbara, she said "Don't let it worry you, we're going on holiday in a couple of days' time, you can leave John in charge, he will look after Jason. I rang Madam and said we would be having a few days off in the school holidays and we will be away, John will be in charge.

"Can you have the boys tomorrow, Thursday?" she not only brought the boys, she had the girl. I felt like I give up being a Keeper and start a children's nursery. I got John to come with me, I made sure I only took one gun, I got the clay pigeon trap out and spent some time on that.

We had to find them some dinner and drink, I took John with me in the afternoon, I would not let them both have guns, I got them back home at three thirty, she was waiting in the yard with Barbara, first thing one of them said, "Mr Rogers would not let both of us have guns," Well, that's up to Mr Rogers, now get in the car and be quiet, she thanked Barbara and asked how Martyn was and again delivered a brown envelope.

We were pleased to get away.

Wally and Peggy made us very welcome again and pleased to see the children and of course the house was empty, he could not help himself but say, "One day you might be living here", Pauline said "We would have a bus going past the gate," Tricia said "Is that the school I will go to!" which was only just down the road, Pauline said "I went to that school a long time ago and Trevor did".

Wally said "It will be up to me who we take on and want your Dad to come and work with me", Peggy said "How do you think about that, Barbara?" that's up to Ted, "But I do think we are being taken a bit for granted, those boys are a bit of a handful".

We had a lovely day at Wallop Air Show watching helicopters and other aircraft and many other places and of course garden centres, which was always a favourite of Barbara's, but the holiday came to an end and we said our goodbyes and again Wally's last words "Don't forget what I told you," I will keep it in mind, and arrived back home about one o'clock.

I pulled up outside the back door and immediately saw the back door was slightly open, I told Barbara to stay in the car. I pushed the door open, my mind went straight to the guns, I ran upstairs and the wardrobe was open and the gun cabinet had been forced open. My gun was still there, the boy's guns were gone.

I phoned the manager at once, also phoned the Boss and Madam. They all arrived at the same time, the Boss asked "What was going on?" the manager explained the boys wanted their guns and I gave into them.

I immediately lost my temper, I thumped him and said "This is a case for the police," Madam took my arm and begged me to calm down, "Ted, we can sort this out," the Boss so enraged he ordered the manager back home to pack his bags and was immediately sacked, I said "You can take my resignation as well," with tears streaming down her face she went to the car, "Barbara, don't let Ted do this, I really don't know what's happened," she got out of the car and the children and went in the house with Madam, the Boss was straight onto the builders to come and repair the damage immediately which they did.

Barbara surprisingly was very calm, she asked Madam if she would mind leaving and let Ted calm down, she knew straight away what was in his mind. Madam said she was very sorry and was clearly upset, we will be back later in the afternoon. Pauline asked if she could help, Mum said "Be a good girl and take the others in the sitting room a while, Dad and I need to talk for a bit," "Can I make you a cup of tea first?" "Oh yes please you're a good girl," she made the tea and made herself scarce with the others.

Barbara sat on the settee and she held Teds hand, I know what you're thinking; he had the phone in the other, "I don't think it's right we should put up with this, what do you think?" "Ted, if that's what you want," he immediately rang his brother Wally, "Hello mate you got home alright," "When can you get a lorry here?" Ted told him part of the reason, "I will ring the Boss straight away, I know he will be happy with that, I will ring you back in less than half an hour." He did so and said his Boss will gladly take me back on and left it with Wally to get a lorry.

We were already packing our bags and boxes, Madam came down late afternoon, the Boss sat in the car and never got out. She came to the door clearly upset, I asked her in. "Ted you don't have to do this, we can get round it, Barbara please stay," "I'm sorry Madam it's too late" and walked into the other room

"Ted, will you bring her back?" she had composed herself a bit when I coaxed Barbara back, she flung her arms round in a big hug and said how sorry they were to let such a thing happen. You're clearly ready to go, "Yes I'm going down to Hampshire to work with my brother," another brown envelope came out of her pocket and pressed it into Barbara's hand, "Thank you for everything you have done for us with tears running down her face," she turned to the door and shook my hand, I opened the door, "Good luck, Ted." Barbara said to me, "She's a very unhappy lady, it makes you wonder what goes on behind closed doors with all their money."

All this going on and we still had Jason, it was a good job he was still only a baby.

Ted's brother Wally and his wife Peggy

Chapter 11

Our Sixth move to Work with Wally

Two days later we were off again on our sixth move, at last we moved into Wally's house and he had moved into the Forester's house, we very soon got unloaded and settled in, I knew the estate program was to clear fell and plant. Every bit had to be rabbit-fenced in. I very soon got back to working with Wally again, social worker came to see Barbara, would she foster again, but we agreed only if they were older children because she had got herself working a few hours at the water cress beds with Wally's wife, and that will fit in with the children's schooling and they were short term fostering.

Pauline had found a friend who loved playing football, her mother Mrs Leggott was trying to get a team together but needed some help, Pauline said she would like to join and mentioned how I was also keen on football and how much I played when I was younger. She asked Pauline if she would ask me to meet and have a talk, and she said she would like that.

I told Pauline to collect Mrs Leggott and the girls together and bring them home for a meeting, I spoke to Barbara about it and she was willing to do the paper work. There was twelve girls turned up they all seemed a pretty eager their ages were between ten and eighteen, Mrs Leggott said she had a kick-about match arranged and would I like to take over, I said "If you want to play regularly, we will have to join the ladies league and you need a proper kit," I asked Mrs Leggott if she would take care of the personal side and if they were able to play each week.

I said "If they were able to pay a sub each week and help raise sum of money, I will see if I can find someone to sponsor us, they will have to rely on their family to transport them around."

We had a nice field in the village which was maintained by the council, I went to see the garage, after a chat he seemed quite keen on the idea for the kit I showed him. The girls had already decided on the name "Abbots Ann Eagles" they were thrilled to bits when I took the kit home, green tops with white shorts and green socks, we ended the season half way up the league which I thought was quite good.

Wally and me were working together very well, we were paid so much an acre to clear fell and replant, timber over a certain size the estate sold on, but we kept all the hazel and chestnut for ourselves which we made into bundles of pea sticks and bean rods and thatching spars and sheep hurdles and in the Shooting season we were asked to Drive the vehicles for the Beater's and Game cart.

Barbara suggested one day that we got room to keep some chickens, I thought about it, I said we might as well get enough. How about if we had a big shed and had them inside, I will have to ask the Boss first, we never saw him very often, he left us to get on with the job.

We were just about to fell a good tree for timber when he turned up and watched us, when it was down he came over to us and said good morning, is this one for the estate. We both said jokingly "yes sir you can have this one," he looked at Wally, "What will this fetch?" then Wally said "Its beech and got a good straight butt I would think it must be close on two hundred pounds and you've got a few down already to be dragged out."

"Now, Ted I'm sorry you were messed about a bit with the house but Wally insisted he wanted you here, Well, I can see you work together perfectly, Wally I see you have some thatching spars and sheep hurdles?" "That's Ted's side line" I never had time before to do it, well, it looks like everything is going alright. "While you're here sir, I would like to ask you something," "Yes, Ted what's that?" "Well, we've got a big garden, have you any objection to me building a sectional shed and keep some chickens?" Well, I will know where I can pick up some fresh eggs every week, what do you think Wally?" "A good idea sir," I think that will be okay, Ted, "Thank you very much sir."

After he had gone Wally said "Where you going to get your shed from?" I said "I will have to buy one I suppose", "Well, how about if I come in with you and build one ourselves? It will have to be big enough to take fifty point of lay pullets" "Well, there's no need to have a floor in it" Wally said "We can cut quite a bit of stuff from our own wood." Barbara and Peggy were thrilled to bits, because we all agreed it will be a joint project between us.

Trevor turned up one day, asked if he could stop for a while, he had met a girl and got a job on a farm as a mechanic, waiting to move in with her which he hoped will not be long, Pauline had got herself a job in Andover, Tricia and Colin were growing up fast, and the fostering had stopped.

We had finished the chicken shed Wally had ordered fifty point of lay pullets to come. When we were building the chicken shed, a chap from the village stood and watched, one day he said, "I could do with a shed like that for a workshop." The birds came and it was not long before we were getting eggs, this Tricia and Colin liked to collect.

Trevor moved out and into the house with his girlfriend on the farm. The girl's football team had been collecting a few pounds with the help of Mrs Leggott for club funds, Barbara had received the list of fixtures for the next season, this meant getting the girls together for a bit of training. Pauline had changed her job on a very big fruit farm where she had met a young man, but she still wanted to play football, this meant a bit more travelling but she got round that by buying herself a scooter.

Our forestry work was going well, but I realised it was all getting a bit too much work, I talked it over with Barbara and she agreed, so I asked Mrs Leggott if she was prepared to take over the football club herself with her husband, they said they will and thanked me for building it up to the standard it was. So we handed everything over books and money, I made sure they signed for everything. I wished them luck but will keep interested all the time Pauline kept playing.

All the time I went to work in the woods I always had the feeling of the of the wildlife around me especially when a cluster of pheasants flew up in front of me, but I knew I had to keep my feet where they were and get on with the job I had, coming up to the third Christmas, I came home. Barbara was waiting for tea time, she was holding a piece of paper with tears in her eyes, gave me the paper, a man from the Ministry.

I could not believe my eyes, owing to the outbreak of fowl pest on the farm at Wallop all poultry within three miles distance of the outbreak had to be destroyed. I phoned Wally immediately, he and Peggy came down straight away, I gave him the paper, well, we are not going to dig that hole ourselves.

He went to the home farm and saw the manager, who we knew and explained the situation and said "I will send a Driver, Tim, up in the morning with a JCB first thing, if you and Ted can be there." He came up the side of the field we had a piece of fence out so he could get close to the shed as possible, he dug the hole out as specified on the paper, he helped Wally and I put up a sheet so we could not be seen from anywhere, to our surprise the local PC called in to say he will sign the paper saying the job had been done, he never stopped, I will call in this evening to see you.

We had the quick lime ready each layer of birds had to be covered, gloves and wellies and a bucket of disinfectant, we had to dispose of every bird. He very soon had the hole out, I could not believe how deep it was, it had to be because it had got to have three foot of soil on top, what a horrible job to do, fifty perfectly good pullets.

The hole was quickly filled, everything cleared, we cleaned up, fence put back, sheet taken down, Tim came in for a cup of tea which Barbara and Peggy had ready for us, and we thanked Tim for his help, he then made his way back to the farm. PC came and signed the form, Wally said "I think we will go now, I will see you in the morning, Ted," we had to explain to Tricia and Colin why we had to get rid of the chickens.

Back to work in the woods we very soon got going as usual, dinner time we sat under a tree and talked, I asked him what we wanted to do with the chicken house, he did not want it and I certainly didn't. I think I had enough of bad luck. I met up with the chap from the village who once said he would like a shed like that, he came and had a look, I cleaned it and disinfected it and left it open, "That's just what I could do with, how much do you want for it?" "You take it down and clear everything you can have it for a hundred and fifty pounds." I was pleased to see it go, he gave me the money and in two days it was gone. I planted some apple trees and plum trees and grassed it over.

That night, back at the yard I gave Wally his half of the money, come in and have a cuppa, while in the house the Phone rang, it was the Boss, he asked if we could be at the river nine o'clock in the morning, we knew just what that was for, it was time for the river to be sorted out. The

Boss was there with the river Keeper and two other men, the boat was put in the water, two men with electrodes to stun the fish and float them to the top and two men to with nets to take out which was not wanted, mainly left was trout, grayling, eels and pike was scooped out and put into dustbins, with the motor providing the electric for the electrodes the boat was pretty heavy.
Wally and I on each bank with a rope each pulling it along, it all went very well together it was a rather slow process, the Boss was pleased with the day.

We were coming up to our third Christmas. Pauline told us she and Tony want to get married in the new year, unfortunately most of the expense fell on our shoulders, not much help from his side, but promised her a good day and a church wedding if that is what she wanted. Time went by and in time they got a council house and she was expecting her first baby, Colin joined the boys football team, we used to go and watch him play when we could.

Wally and I had a heavy morning plus the rain we were very wet, he suggested we pack up dinner time, we loaded our tools on the trailer and drove the tractor towards home, he made himself comfortable sitting down. I came to the cross roads where I had to stop before turning, I looked round he was sitting down, we put our thumbs up to say we were all right, a car was following behind, I could see it was an air force man driving behind from Wallop air base.
 I looked round again and Wally had fell out onto the road, I stopped and ran back to him, the chap in the car had stopped. I immediately saw Wally was in trouble, blood trickled from his ear, the chap in the car had already sent for an ambulance which was here in minutes and quickly loaded in and off to Winchester hospital, they had phoned

the police and RTA, interviewed the chap in the car who saw just what had happened and cleared me of any involvement. I had permission from the police to turn the tractor round and Drive a few minutes back to my house. Barbara had just come home, I told her what had happened, "I must go and get Peggy and go straight to the hospital" she gave me a kiss, "please be careful, give me a ring when you can," I will and drove off to pick Peggy up.

It seemed to take hours to get there but in fact it took less than half an hour we found the reception and gave all the particulars, a doctor came to talk to us, he said Wally had a slight skull fracture, but might have other complications, at the moment he is in emergency care, but you can see him for a few moments, the doctor said we have rooms for relatives to stay overnight. I realised I still had my working cloths on, Peggy said she would like to stay overnight, I said "I will go back and change", she asked "if Barbara will go up and collect a few things she will know what I want."

Colin and Tricia had to come home from school, so we had to tell them what we were doing, I told Barbara "I might sit by him all night if I have to." I had a bag with Peggy's clothes, she asked the nurse if she could have a room, this is his brother, he would like to sit with him, they brought a comfy chair for me, we sat with him.

Peggy sat with us but then said she had to get some sleep. The nurse took her to a room with a drink. It was quite comfy in my chair, the nurse brought me a coffee, I sat looking at him and trying to fathom out why he fell off the trailer.

The nurse came in a number of times through the night, in the morning the doctor came and removed some of the wires and pipes, but told me he was still very ill. Peggy came in, I asked her if she would like some breakfast, they had a café we can use, not that we felt like much, I said to Peggy I will have to go home and sort a few thing out, but I will be back tonight, I left her some money so she could get something to eat or drink.

When I got home I phoned the police, explained who I was and asked if it was possible to talk to the officer who was in charge of the accident. They said we can find him and send him out. Barbara had taken the tools out of the trailer and put away in my shed. I went back into the hospital, didn't know what to expect he was still in intensive care, I saw the doctor and said he thought there was slight improvement, only time will tell. Peggy stopped another night, I told her I will work tomorrow and see you tomorrow night.

I was up in the morning and said goodbye to Tricia. Colin and Martyn who were coming up to three years old, they held my hand and said "Uncle Wally will be alright won't he?" I said "Yes he will get better," Barbara gave me a kiss "Please be careful don't be late home," I promise, I won't. I was well into work when I heard someone shout, I could see it was the police car, "Mr Rogers, I got a message you want to see me," "Yes I wondered if you could give me any light what happened to my brother at the scene of the accident, because I am still baffled as to why he fell out of the trailer".

"Well, let me put your mind at rest, it was an air force officer following you and gave us a full statement as to what happened. It was clearly not your fault, for some reason your brother stood up and lost his balance and that was it," Well, I know the weather was damned awful. He shook my hand and told me not to worry and hoped my brother will be home soon.

By now I had enough so I decided to pack up and go home, I was home before Barbara. She was doing a few hours at the water cress beds, I had washed and changed and sat on the settee when she came in, she came straight to me and kissed me and a big cuddle and said "it wasn't your fault now stop blaming yourself." I said "I try and get hold of the Boss, I left a message for him to say, if he was coming this way I would like to see him."

It wasn't for a few days when he came and found me working, I had just felled decent sized beech and trimming it out, I put the saw down, he said "Good morning Ted, come and sit down," we both perched ourselves on the tree I had felled, "I am sorry to hear about Wally now what I have heard it was clearly not your fault but I want you to promise me, if you feel like packing up you will stop work and go home, if there is anything you or Wally's wife need, you go and get it whatever it is, I will write to her and when Wally is feeling much better I will go and see him," I thanked him very much and he was on his way.

I went in and saw Wally and Peggy was sat beside him she said he had opened his eyes twice but no reaction from him, I held his hand but no response, I told her I had seen the Boss and he said he will be in touch with her. Christmas was just around the corner and Wally had begun to react to certain things, but there was no way he was going to be home for some time.

I was still required to drive the tractors for shoot days which pulled on the Shooting strings a bit, I brought Peggy home before Christmas. They had two daughters and a son so they started to take it in turns in travelling back and forth to the hospital.

Pauline came and had a couple of days with us we all kept as cheerful as we could.

Christmas over, Wally had made a lot of improvement he had begun to sit up for a while but not taking much notice, the Boss kept his word and went to see Wally and was very upset to see how ill he was. I asked the doctor if he will recover enough to work again, he shrugged his shoulders, who knows, I asked him if he might have any idea why he stood up in the trailer that day when there was no need to. "We know by what you have told us it was a pretty awful wet morning and a very hard working one, when he gets a little better we will see if there is any underlying reason for that to happen."

Colin had left school now and had a little job with a family making leather cases and drum kits, he was also keen on Shooting, it was in his blood but he wasn't old enough to have a licence, but at the last place we were at, he used to use a twenty bore and do a bit of clay Shooting. I still had my one gun. As he got a bit older and stronger he began to use my gun, Barbara used to love taking him around different clay Shoots. Tricia had another year to go to school, she did like her hairdressing and liked singing to Martyn.

Wally began to move around a bit more it was a long time before he came home, it was clear to me that he was never going to be able to do the same kind of work and work alongside with me, which I was sad to see every day. The Boss came to see Peggy and could see they had a bed made up down stairs for him when he did come home. He asked her how she felt about moving into a bungalow, there was one coming vacant shortly, he was quite willing to have it made accessible for anyone disabled, she asked the son and daughters what they thought and if it was to their liking.

They agreed it would be for the best. Peggy rang the estate office and agreed to move they told her the Boss had already ordered the alterations to go ahead and will try and finish to coincide, so Wally will be able to go straight in. I tried to help as much as I could, but still had to keep the work going in the woods but finding it was more harder on my one man tree felling and carrying out the cord wood was not an easy job on your own. When I next saw the Boss I mentioned it to him, all he said was, "Well, just carry on the best you can," as time went on, Barbara could see I was doing too much and was not enjoying the job at all and was not happy.

I was working, when a car come up the wide ride. I could not recognise my own car, but I did the person who got out it was Barbara, I thought 'Oh not bad news,' "What are you doing here?" "Well, there's no one at home for a while so I've brought my dinner to have with you," Let's sit under the tree I felled yesterday.

"I want to finish this one this afternoon some of those pieces of wood are far too big to carry, well, it's all got to be staked up, it's going to be difficult to work out the money side of it." She said "I will help you," "Well, I don't want to take on another section of woodland like this anyway," she said "I know what's in your mind let's talk it over tonight, I had better get on again," she gave me a kiss, "Be careful I will see you later."

I was a bit late getting home but I finished the tree, we sat down. Colin went out playing football on the green. Tricia done he usual thing reading a story to Martyn, so we able to sit quietly and talk over our past and where we've got to now. She said "would you like to go back to Keepering again," "Well, it won't be such heavy work I didn't mind the long hours and would not have a chainsaw rattling in my ears all day."

The next couple of weeks Barbara took in the Shooting Times, there was a small advert in the second week, 'Single-handed Keeper required mid of season for future small estate Linley Bishops Castle,' Well, I presume they haven't reared any birds this years, it might be interesting to find out.

Barbara smiled at me "It's Saturday tomorrow, give them a ring in the morning," this I did and spoke to Mr Jackson,

I said I was enquiring about the Keeper's job that was advertised and my name was Mr Rogers. He said he was responsible for the syndicate and one thing he asked "if Mrs Rogers would be able to cook the lunch for about fifteen people this will be something we would like to have," I said "that would not be a problem she has done that sort of thing before." He told me he had seen two others but said I will not be taking them on, "Would you like to come for an interview, does that sound all right to you, shall we say a fortnight today at eleven o'clock,?" "Yes thank you very much". He gave me the address, School House, Linley, Bishops Castle, "I'll look forward to meeting you." I put the phone down, I can't believe it, Barbara, said "What can't you believe?" Well, he wants us to go for an interview in two weeks' time, where is the map?" We don't know where it is so with a bit of excitement we found it, it's up in Shropshire do you want to go up there, well it will be a part of the country we have not been to.

So when I got back, next week I won't fell any big timber, I will do what orders I got for hurdles and spars and see what happens in two weeks' time. Barbara went to see Pauline and have a coffee with her and told her what we were doing, If I come and get you on Friday night so we can get a good start Saturday morning, Tricia always looks forwards to seeing her big sister.

We got away early and arrived at Bishops Castle. Barbara said we could do with a drink, we were surprised how small the town was, it was a kind of oldie-worldly place but seemed quite nice.

We found a little café and had a coffee and a bite to eat, the lady asked if we had come far, it must have been our accents that gave us away, we said we were looking for a place called Linley, "Any particular place?" "Yes, I said, The school house," "Oh that's on Jasper Moore's estate that's the Game Keeper's house," we smiled at each other and thanked her, she said "If you go up the hill out of town, turn right keep going, you go over the little bridge, immediately on your right on the bank is the house."

It was just as she said and up the Drive was a Land Rover, we both got out and a gentleman came out of the house, "Mr and Mrs Rogers?" "Yes, Mr Jackson," "Well, you timed that about right, I have just put the kettle on, come in as well, Mrs Rogers this is the house, shall we have a cup of tea and a chat?" I said I'm Ted and this is Barbara, "Well, this year as a syndicate, we thought we would try something different, we are willing to buy in a thousand poults to release in pens, we have an incubator, how do you feel about that?" "Well, there's two ways to look at it, if you hatch your own or buy in day olds, there's always a risk of losing a certain amount, but with poults you start with a good birds." "Would you be happy to have poults this year," "Yes I would."

"Now Barbara Ted told me you have cooked big meals before, if we gave you a curtain amount each week to buy food in and cook for about fifteen on Shoot day," "Yes I can do that," we'll have a look round the house and then we'll have a look at the other part of the house, we went outside and adjoining the house was the old school, the first room had the incubator, through the door was the school room which had a very large fire place, Barbara said "This is the room you want the meals served, can I suggest we have one long table for you all to sit at and a large fire going not only for lunch time but when you come in at the end of the day?

Can I ask if you will agree on Shoot days I organise the whole day so that will take any pressure off you to enjoy the day with your friends," "Well, I must admit it will be a total turn round to what we have been doing. Why not

I'm sure the rest of the party will love it."
"Now let's jump in the Land Rover and I will take you up the valley, the river runs right up the middle with woods on both sides running right to the top of the hills," Ted said can I see some real sporting birds here, "Well, I like to think we have a good team of guns."
"On our way back down, there is one favourite Drive I like, you see the little thatched cottage, well that is Driven out of the valley, if you get out and stand, you will get a better idea, but my way of thinking we haven't got it quite right," "Well, you have got a small release pen opposite," "No we've only two pens one at each end of the valley!, "Feed the birds behind the cottage and Drive them back home," "Right, with that suggestion I would like to offer you and Barbara the job as the Linley Game Keeper."
"Thank you very much" We both shook hands, he looked at his watch. "Now I would like to take you back in the town and treat you to lunch and we can talk a few things over then. Barbara said thank you very much Mr Jackson. "You get your car and follow me," we followed him to a nice hotel and talked over lunch, I asked him about the big house just inside the Drive, "the estate belongs to Sir Jasper Moore, he has nothing to do with the Shoot, the sheep run right up the length of the valley, I give the farm manager the Shoot dates a couple of days before he runs the sheep right back out of the valley".
"You have two sons and a daughter to come with you", "Yes the oldest one will look for a job, and the daughter will be leaving school shortly", there is a school bus that comes this way for the younger boy.

"Now Ted, you are more or less self-employed, so what sort of notice will you give?" "Well, how soon do you want me to start?" "Will two weeks today move you here?, I will order a removal van, it may be they will arrive on

Friday afternoon, I'll give them your address," and in return he gave me fifty pounds for travelling expenses, we shook hands and both thanked him for the lunch, and we look forward to seeing you again.

We were on our way back home, Barbara could not believe what we were doing, once again there was always something exciting about moving and meeting other people and we were going to tell the children all about our day away.

Much to our surprise we arrived home about seven o'clock so there was plenty of time to tell them about today before bedtime, Colin said "I will have to find a job," Ted told him but you will be able to do more Shooting and Tricia said "I will go to a new school before I leave and get a job," and she said "Martyn will go to a new school." Pauline said "You're all going to leave me behind" and Tricia said "We will see you again" they both cuddled and said "Well, you can come and have a holiday with us," Martyn had already gone to bed.

We will have to go and see Peggy and put her in the picture, I believe Wally will soon be out of hospital and the bungalow was ready for them to go into.

We met up with Peggy and she told us they had decided to move house and take Wally straight there, I said "we'll come and see you before we go," she was sorry we were going but understood why. I had told the Boss, he came to see me and had a chat, I told him how I felt about the situation I was in, he said get in touch with the office and they will sort your money and everything out for you.

It was not long ago we were in touch with our last social worker at Shrewsbury and when Barbara rang her, she was pleased to hear from us, when she knew the address, we were going to she said that's not far from me, I will come and see you after you've moved in with good news. To us that could only mean one thing, to us she has our baby however you look at it, .I had a chap come and look at my hurdles and spars and bits and pieces, when I told him I was finishing he quickly bought everything I had. I went to the wood on Friday morning for the last time and secretary came to find me, I have brought your money and everything else you are entitled to, we were all very upset when Wally was ill, but everybody wishes you and Barbara the best for the future. I took the tractor and tools back to the yard and walked back home past the dreaded spot for the last time.

It was a good job we had a big gate into the garden, the lorry was already backed up to the house, Barbara had made the two men a cuppa and I was ready for a drink they had already asked Barbara if they can put some of the furniture in the lorry, it's a good idea because it will save a lot of time in the morning. They asked if there was a pub close by where they could get a meal, Barbara said I can knock you up something, "Oh no, that's alright we will try not to disturb you when we come back. The pub is just down the road."

Chapter 12

Bishops Castle

We were off to another house and new job which will be our seventh move.

We had our tea and packed a few more things carried some boxes down stairs, Mum said "Right that's enough, let's have a sit down and have a chat, Jason the dog was always thought of and this is where he was going to do his work, he was always happy in this house, this is where he will stay.

We were up early next morning and we had a quick breakfast, lorry men as well, they loaded the last bits of furniture on, the doors closed, the lorry ticking over and ready to go. Ted closed the big garden gate, Barbara asked shall I Drive, the answer was a big yes, and Martyn shouted follow that lorry, there was still the questions 'what is this like' ' what is that like' which helped to pass the time by. Colin said "We have just passed the sign saying Bishops Castle," Oh well, it won't be long now, the minute we go over the little river bridge the lorry slowed down here it is, we followed up the Drive behind and pulled up, Jason was as bad as the children, could not get out quick enough to have a look round.

A lady from just up the road called out, Ted went to see her, "Mr and Mrs Rogers, Mr Jackson asked if I will keep an eye open for you and give you the key, my name is Barbara Butler," "Well, there's a coincidence my name is Barbara," she said "Please give us a shout if you need anything, you will want some milk, I will bring you some down." She ran off and the lorry was already being unloaded with the garden stuff.

Tricia had done her job of keeping Martyn amused Colin

was a great help, Barbara Butler came down with a jug of fresh milk and would not accept anything for it, it was nearly four o'clock and the lorry had gone, we were all exploring the house and the old school room. Before we left the other house, the postman had given us the mail and never looked at it until now.

Was this something uncanny, they said John had applied for a job close to Bishops Castle, as Game Keeper, a place called Lydham, and will be moving in two weeks' time, Tricia could not believe her god parents were coming to live close to us. We had just started to sort a few more things out, when two Land Rovers pulled up the Drive, to our surprise it was Mr Jackson and one of the syndicate, "Ted, I would like you to meet Mr Edwards, you see we have brought two Land Rovers the one at the back is for you to use, we will allow you an amount of money in your wages for fuel.

Have a good look round when you get settled in and assess where, if any, we can improve the Shoot, can I have a word with Barbara?" she came to the door, "Barbara, when you get settled I will come to see you again to see what pots and pans and cutlery we are going to need. I will pop round in due course."

In the middle of the week we had a phone call from the social worker asking if she could come one evening which will be on the Wednesday, Barbara told me to be calm, she knew I was angry to think we had to wait twelve years or more to go to court to get the final signature to this adoption form. I sat quiet with Tricia hold our hands, "I can assure you there is no problem, all you have to do is go into the judge's chambers, he will ask you if you know what this means to Tricia, Barbara you will be asked to pay five pounds fee. He will sign it and you will be able to come home." Colin was old enough to look after Martyn and Barbara Butler from up the road said she would keep an eye on them, we did not discuss the reason why.

Back home we resumed everything just the same, after tea Barbara was in the kitchen I saw Tricia go up to her and said "Now I am a Rogers," Mum said Darling you always have been and you always will be." After having a good look round, Barbara could see that she was going to have to have some help on Shoot days, she had a word with Barbara Butler who was only too pleased to help, it was made clear to her she will be paid, her husband Frank was also pleased to help on Shoot days. He worked on the estate so he knew the layout of the woods quite well. Colin was still doing his clay shooting and met up with a chap who had his own building business and was looking for a young lad to help him and offered Colin a job, learning to do brick laying and wood work and his yard was only just up the road from us.

Barbara had planned out the kind of set-up she would like. the most important thing was a hot oven on wheels so they could wheel it round from the house to the Shoot room so the meals will be piping hot, we also had our big old iron pot which would hang over an open fire for the special Keeper's soup. Tricia was about to leave school in a few weeks, but went to school for a week or two mainly to take Martyn on the bus which stopped outside the gate.

I had already been putting the pens ready to put poults in and found some wire to make small pens opposite the thatched cottage. I knew I would have to get another dog so I set to and re-built the kennels, I always made sure the beds were up off the floor and a small shed suitable for the Beaters.

Colin started work building and other jobs, Tricia left school and got a job in a chicken factory at Craven Arms which sent a bus round the villages to pick up the workforce and quickly made friends with two girls living not too far away from us. It was not long before the birds were due to come, Barbara ask me if she could help release them, another pair of hands always helps. Frank Butler told me about a chap who lives in Bishops Castle, Jack Bush, he works in the wood yard and has a couple of good dogs and as a hobby does a few days picking up, if you like I will see him tomorrow and get him to come and see you, you might be able to do a deal with him for some odd bits of wood that you want for tables and seating".

Frank said "If you like, Ted, I will give you a hand to put it together, well, with you and your Barbara helping, it's a big help and will see you get recompensed for it somehow." Colin helped me work out how we could put some wood together, make some trestles and ply board for the tables.

That evening a tractor pulled up in the Drive, Frank got out with someone else, "Hi, Ted I've brought you a load of offcuts and rubbish and this is Jack Bush, the chap I told you about," "Hello Jack, I've heard you do a bit of picking up in the season, well, I'm sure we can do with someone to do that job."

"Now Frank what have you got on this trailer? Colin will give a lift off with it," he whispered in my ear, "Dad there's some good stuff on here," "What do you do with rubbish Jack?" "Well, if you don't have it, it will only go on the bonfire," Frank said "Well, I reckon we can do something with it Ted, right, let's get it off, then we'll go in and have a cuppa."

It was Frank's tractor from the farm which he worked on, he took the tractor back, I told him call back in, I knew Frank would. When we sorted through the heap of wood it was surprising how much good pieces we picked out and carried it into the old school room ready to put together some for the tables and some for the seats and some of the smaller pieces were stacked at the side of the old fire place.

Frank came down and remarked how much this was going to look better than before and it was not long before we had finished. Barbara set to and found some big old table cloths and covered the tables "wow" she said "I think we can all be proud of that, I wonder what Mr Jackson will say when he sees it? There's one thing we haven't lit the fire yet" Frank said "We can very soon put that to the test" and in no time had flames up the chimney and heat coming out into the room.

We ought to find a fire guard Colin said "I know where there's one, up in the corner of the garden there's a piece of fencing" and he went up and got it between us we bent it and knocked it into shape it fit perfectly.

We just settled down in the evening the phone rang Tricia answered, "Hello!" she shouted "Its Aunty Nell, Mum's here, yes we have been pretty busy, I'll hand you over," in a long chat the outcome was, "Can we come and stay once again? We still have our Camper van this next week" "You know you're always welcome we look forward to seeing you, we have a lot to talk about."

I had a walk up the valley with Jason mulling over in my mind this that and the other and leaning on the little foot bridge that went across the river, when a Land Rover pulled up, it was the Boss, he came to me smiling, "Have you got it all worked out, Ted?" I said "I can't see as I can do much more until the birds come," "Barbara told me where I could find you, shall we go back to the house and have a chat, I want a word with Barbara as well," he opened the back door and Jason was very soon up and in. Back at the house, Barbara was in the old school room, "I'm in here," she called out, "You had better come in here first," the Boss laughed "goodness me what have you been doing here?" Barbara said "Well, I hope you like it," "I certainly like this long table and the benches." "I will dish the meals up in the house, put them in the hot oven, and transfer them into here. I will have my friend from up the road to come and help me, you can see on the fire a very large pot for a constant soup on the go, you can have a bowl full before lunch and it can be served when you come in at the end of the day, but I will need to know how many there will be for lunch." "Barbara, I will ask my wife to be responsible for that first thing, I am looking forward to this season especially the cooked dinners, now I will be off on holiday tomorrow so I won't see you until before the next Shoot," "Well, the birds come next Wednesday, so we'll be busy then!" "Right, I will say goodbye and wish you luck," we shook hands, he was in his Land Rover and away.

Tricia helped Mum in the evenings after work as she needed it, Colin also liked to get involved, the birds arrived nice and early Wednesday, two men from the Game farm came and Barbara opened the crates and let them out, we carried them in and emptied out most in the big pens, with just a few in the small one. It was a trial spot opposite the thatched cottage.

When the time came to call and feed them back across the valley and Drive them back home to their pens, I had already put food and water in, I didn't know she had brought her clicker. As she let them out, she counted them and told me there was twelve extra, their Boss had told them to tell me, but they had forgot, job done they were on their way.

Barbara and I went back to the first pen and pleased to see some of them had found the food and even found some of the perches. The sooner you get them off the ground the better. I feed three times a day, as time went by I could see a number of older birds were showing, which I was pleased about, but could not make out where they're coming from, I did not mention this to anyone, I did tell

Barbara and "Well, we will see at the end of the day," Colin came to me, "I asked him if he was alright with the dog," " Yes, I'm alright, give us about fifteen minutes to get up to the top of the next Drive," the Boss will go with Colin when he is ready.

We lined out at the top of the hill, whistle went and there were birds going everywhere, forwards, back, behind, someone's dog going berserk, I stooped the line on a small path and a few choice words in the right direction. The dog back under control, we moved on, went as far as the wide fire break where she said "That's a good thing isn't it" It's a good job I got the Boss to bring a load of corn offal from his drier mixed with grower's pellets, Colin helped a lot on Shoot days he helped put the pegs out for the guns to stand to.

The first day came round very quick, I had the fire going in the school room, I lit the old oil burner in the small shed for the Beaters, Barbara Butler came down early to help, and she had not done anything like this before but was very eager to help.

The big old iron pot was on the edge of the fire with the soup warming nicely. The Boss was first with his wife, she immediately told Barbara there will be sixteen for lunch.

Barbara had to show Tricia how to serve a bowl of soup as soon as they came in, and of course the bottles very soon appeared on the table. The Boss came and gave me the money for the Beaters.

I had already agreed for them to be on their pegs at nine thirty, they had drawn their peg numbers and moved to up to each Drive, three Drives in the morning and two in the afternoon, they can walk to the morning Drives, the Boss asked "Have you got someone to take us to our pegs?" "Yes, Colin will do that"

I had fed them across the valley behind the thatched

cottage, Frank had taken the Beaters up the road well, away from the Drive and waited for me to catch them up. Jack Bush was in position for picking anything that was well behind the guns although they never all had dogs, I let
Colin have Jason which worked out perfectly well, I waited for whistle. Colin had to remind the Boss that it was his job to start. At last we were slowly on our way, I had to slow the line down once or twice, it could not have gone better, and the Drive ended when I blew my whistle and gathered the Beaters together to wait before going on. The Boss came over, "Well, Ted you got that spot on," some of the guns were stood and others round the corner, I blew the whistle. I asked Frank if he would take the Beaters to the far end of the fire break and wait for me there.
This last Drive before lunch, Colin was still helping pick up, I knew he would see where to come. I took the party on, this time the pegs were well in site along the edge of the valley with the big house in sight, it was a beautiful spot. Unbeknown to anyone else only Colin, I had acquired a two-way Walky Talky radio which linked up to Frank. With my fingers crossed, I called him, I was stood close to the Boss, he jokingly said "Are we on army manoeuvres Ted?"
A shot rang out at the end of the line, someone said "woodcock," you could see the birds coming down from the top of the hill with plenty of air under their wings. They lifted high over the guns to reach the other side of the valley, this is where I spotted the older birds early on in the season. I had asked Colin's Boss to follow behind with my Land Rover to carry the Game, it may be because he was late turning up, but he caught up with us and Colin. I heard the Boss say "Lunch time gentlemen," a nice slow walk back to the house where Barbara was ready with

soup if they wanted before lunch, she had even thought of putting a bowl and a jug of hot water to wash their hands and a towel.

Barbara and her friend served the lunches and of course heard a lot of comments how good the morning went. I went in just as they were clearing the main plates and Barbara was asking who would like a pudding, Tricia and Martyn had brought them round in the hot oven and Barbara Butler was ready to dish them out. Nobody refused, but gave a rousing cheer to all of them.

I had a quick word with the Boss if he will take the party in the vehicles and Colin will tell you where to park up and you won't have far to walk to your pegs. "We will walk a part of the down land into the woods so be prepared for a covey of partridge, we will wait for your whistle."

Frank had left his tractor and trailer so he used it to take the Beaters right round the top of the hill then left it at the gateway to the valley, then joined in with us. Colin once again knew what to do, the hill itself was covered in blue berries and heather, I had seen the odd partridge but suddenly a huge covey got up and they split, some went round the hill and by the response of the Shooting, I guessed some went down the valley with the odd pheasant, we got to the edge of the wood and lined up again, and walked slowly down the hill.

I kept the line as slow as I could because we only wanted to do one more Drive, which was almost opposite this one across the valley. After we pulled out and gathered together Colin came to me and whispered, "Dad we have cleared over a hundred, I asked the Boss to give us a quarter of an hour before he got to his pegs."

Walking up and down the hills, it had been a tiring day for the Beaters, but eventually brought the day to an end, last Drive over. Frank had loaded everyone on board, all birds picked up and hung in my Land Rover. All in convoy,

Drive down the valley to home and in by the big fire. Martyn, Tricia and the ladies were there to make sure they all had a bowl of soup if they wanted. I paid the Beaters their money and off they went home. Frank and Colin pickers up, helped hang the birds in the Beaters shed, when that was done Colin took them in the house for a drink.

In the traditional way, I sorted a brace of birds for each gun and took them in for each one to have, if this was a private Shoot, I would have received a tip from each one, but you did not get it from a syndicate that came through our wages. But they all shook hands and said what a wonderful day, especially when I told them the bag was one hundred and twenty six pheasants, eight partridge, two woodcock and of course they were really over the moon about the lunch which they already had rewarded Barbara for.

After they had all had a good old chat and departed and emptied a few bottles, if it had not been for the wives driving, some of them would not have got home! The Boss came to the door with his wife and came in, the first thing she said, "Barbara you must give me your soup recipe, it was absolutely beautiful," I asked him what he wanted to do with the Game, "Can I leave that with you Ted?" "I will take it first thing Monday morning to the dealer in town."

Well, that was the first day over, Barbara was pleased with her side of the day and she gave Tricia and Martyn something for their help. Up the next day Sunday or not, the birds had to be fed. Nell and Reg turned up in their Camper Van they soon made their selves at home and we had plenty to talk about and tidy up the old school room. They were surprised to see how Tricia and Martyn had grown up, Reg was keen to come with me feeding, I had put a number of self-feeders, so I was not surprised to see a lack of response to my whistle, but knew they will be back, after a Shoot it takes a while for them to settle down.

Pauline rang, she had her second baby. Barbara was a bit upset, I could tell she wasn't very happy, "If Dad and I come down and get you next weekend," "I will tell Bryan, he can go and live with his Mum for a week," she said "he might as well go for good because he is never here, Jennie's coming round to stop with me tonight," she was one of the girls who played football with her, "I must ring off now, thanks for paying for the call Mum" "You know you can call anytime, see you next Saturday, bye now."
Nell looked up, now there's a coincidence, we were going to ask if we could stop another week, Colin said "Dad why don't you go down on the Friday? I can feed round the week end," Reg said "I can help also," But don't forget we Shoot that following weekend. Somehow we will have to take Pauline home" "No problem" Reg said "We can take her home on our way down and that will give us another couple of days here and I would love to have a day's beating with you, Ted." Martyn being Nell's favourite, Tricia sitting with them said "You will be able to help serve the lunches, won't you Aunty Nell? with a large fire."
"Colin, will you take a brace of birds for your Boss in the morning? When I come back from feeding I will take the rest of the birds to the dealers," Reg said "I will come with you Ted."
Pauline rang on Wednesday and was thrilled when her Mum told her "We will be down on Friday and we will book into a Bed and Breakfast before we come to you, and we will bring you back with us for a week, see you on Friday bye for now."
We booked in Bed and Breakfast and asked for an early

breakfast, but first went and found Pauline and told her everything what happened while we have been there, she was pleased to hear about Tricia. "Now, is there anything you want? We've got time to go into town and get a few things" Mum knowing she will want some things for the two boys, in and out of the shops buying this and that, Barbara was in her element and finally back to Pauline's for tea, just as we got there Jenny arrived, "You going to stop for tea Jenny? It's lovely to see you both," With a kiss and of course the ladies' football team came in the conversation. But had both finished with that, and Jenny was into playing darts and gradually getting Pauline interested so much, that she had bought herself a dart board and both played at home.

Pauline having the two boys that was the best they could do but both were keen players, their plan was to join a darts club each, taking it in turn to sit with Pauline's boys. Jenny visited Pauline often, they were good friends, they packed a few things ready for morning.

It was time to say goodnight, Jenny only lived just round the corner, I have a key so I will look after the flat, Barbara said if you ring us please reverse the charges.

We got away in good time in the morning that allowed us two stops on the way, we arrived home just after dinner as soon as we stopped, Pauline was out of the car and straight into Tricia's arms. It was so good to see them a lot of fuss made all round.

Weekend over, it was time to think about the next Shoot, feeding to do every day, and still those extra birds coming in from somewhere. With the self-feeders working well, the birds were spreading out a bit more. This meant finding at least two more Drives and the idea would be to leave one good Drive till last if you were having a bad day. I found another route for Frank to take the tractor round the top of the hill, to drop the Beater off, I pegged the stands for the guns. Ted always talked the Shoot over with Colin, so he was in charge of the Boss telling them where to go and stand.

Tricia and Colin worked all day but joined the fun at night, Martyn clung to his Aunty Nell, Tricia and Pauline inseparable, Reg liked a Game of crib with Barbara and the two grandsons had their toy to play with.

Barbara Butler came down on Thursday and Friday to prepare some of the food and dishes for Saturday, she could only guess there will be the same for lunch as last time but from past experience always had that bit extra. Frank and I made sure the Walky Talkies were working because the first Drive was going to be a long one, the Boss and his wife were first to arrive and went in the house to see Barbara and of course met the rest of the family.

"There will be one more today Barbara, let me have the bill later, Ted here's the Beaters' money", "Thank you, now are you happy for Colin to show you to your pegs?" "Yes indeed we are, yes, I don't know what we would have done without him, and how we ever went on without Frank and his tractor and trailer." "Well, I must warn you the first Drive starts the other end of the hill, so there's no telling what comes down and along the line of the valley. It can play tricks with birds."

"May I ask what's for lunch?" "Yes roast lamb," "Oh I can almost taste it already. Right we will go and unload," Barbara asked Tricia if she will go in the Shoot room and see if there's anything they want. Pauline went in with her, she chucked another lump of wood on the fire, it was quite safe with the fire guard, the Boss and Mrs came in, Tricia said I must go and get another setting, she came back in, "Thankyou Tricia, we must say you are all very well organised," Pauline said "We have to be with Mum and

Dad in charge of the family!"

We must go now, the rest of the party are coming, Colin took charge of the draw for the pegs and to walk them down to the first Drive, he had Frank's radio for this Drive so he was in contact with me, it was a long way to the end of the wood plus taking part of the down land in, we line' out along the track and waited quietly. At last Colin's radio crackled. We're in position, there was a lot of open grass land before we got to the real woodland and then it was a bit harder going, I did have some self-feeders on the open grass patches and some of them were being used.

I was pleased to hear the whole line were getting some Shooting, I slowed the line down, we were well, in time, it took Frank a while to go right the way round to pick the Beaters up to take them on again. This was going to be a long Drive again, I saw Colin and left him in charge and we moved on, I had no idea what would turn up on this Drive, but by the Shooting it sounded pretty good , one more before lunch, Colin took them in their Rovers to a small clearing out of sight and walked back to their line of pegs, the Boss asked Colin, "Have we got time for a quick drink," the bottle was already going round, "No you've not" he said jokingly, knowing it would be a while before the Beaters were ready, "they won't start until you blow your whistle."

Once started, it was only a short Drive but somehow the birds were reluctant to fly at first, this was because some old wire netting was left there which I had not seen before, but as they started to run round it, a good many took off and went forward and not a bad result after all.

I blew the whistle and it was back home for lunch, there was always a buzz of excitement, they were a jovial lot of men together especially when Barbara and staff arrived with the food, followed up with sponge pudding and custard, tea or coffee or with their own drink, the old iron soup pot was on the side of the fire if needed.

On our way out going past the big house I saw two young men in the garden, I had seen them before walking up the valley, so I thought I would find out who they might be, I asked the farm manager the next time I saw him, he wasn't sure himself, but heard they lived in London and were related to the family and will take ownership in time.

My old Dad used to say, you don't know what's round the corner' so I tried to put all thoughts out of my mind.

Lunch over and on our way to two more Drives to finish the day, the bag was better than I thought I met up with Colin he said he had a good day with Jason the dog, he picked up really well, the bag was one hundred and fifteen, back in the Shoot room they were all very pleased with the day. I spoke to the Boss, the next day will be the fourth day we have shot just before Christmas.

I asked him if he wanted a good day, "Yes Ted why not? I think we will have a few more for lunch, I must come in and settle up with Barbara," he asked his wife to come in as well, she said "have you all had a lovely week?" "Yes, we have, sadly we're all going home on Monday" Pauline said "Aunty and Uncle are taking us down and dropping us at the door," "Well, I am sure we will see you again shortly, now, Barbara can you cope with twenty of us next time?" "Oh I'm sure we will and we will make it a special one," "Thank you all for a lovely day."

Barbara set ourselves one hour to clear some of the mess up and then we will go in the other room and finish the rest tomorrow. Ted said "I think we all deserve a drink, there's some sherry and whatever else you like." Then Aunty Nell said "Now, I have a little surprise for you, you all know Uncle David, how he flew these Jet Planes in the Air Force. He knows we will be leaving on Monday morning, he is based in South Wales so precisely at eight thirty he will fly over," Martyn said "how does he know where we are?" she said "Well, he has a very clever airplane, he can find anything he wants," Pauline said "He's planned this," Nell said "Yes, this will be part of his days' work".

On Sunday we got together and very soon got back to normal, Nell helped Barbara with the lunch, Pauline and Tricia and Martyn had fun and Games with Pauline's two youngsters and walked up the road and told Barbara Butler what was going to happen in the morning, I will make sure the children come down to your house and catch the bus.

Tricia said "I will miss him", Mum said "No you won't because you can have tomorrow off," we didn't know that Nell had already told Barbara what was going to happen, so she rang the factory and explained the situation and they were quite happy for her to have that day off, off her holiday, "Oh Mum, thank you."

They loaded the Camper Van up ready for the morning, there was no trouble to get anybody up next morning. All had breakfast and loaded up all ready to go, we all waiting outside and surprised to see other children on the road waiting so the word had got round, suddenly Reg said "I can hear him coming over there look!" and dead on time coming straight at us and thundered over and straight up the valley and sure enough, we saw him go round and line us up again, but he was not going so fast, as he went over he dipped his wing, which we knew he could see us and say goodbye, Nell and Reg were so proud of him we all waved as he disappeared up the valley and out of sight.

The school bus was on time, Martyn said his goodbye to everybody and got on board with the others. Nell and Reg said goodbye, Tricia and Pauline hung onto each other and the Grand children could not wait to get in the van, kisses all round, Pauline promised to keep in touch and will come up again.

Back to normal, Barbara was already working on this being a Christmas Shoot, so Tricia and Martyn helped by making paper chains and hung them round the Shoot Room and house. A surprise phone call came from Pauline saying she had booked on a coach to come up to Bishops Castle on the Wednesday before the Shoot, arriving in the afternoon, will give you a ring when we get there.

We made a point to go and find our friends John Blackburn and his wife who moved to a Shoot not far away, we went on the weekend so Colin, Tricia and Martyn, could come and see them, and what a greeting we had! There was so much to talk about, he had his own Shoot to think about, he was pleased when I asked him to come and pick up on our special Christmas Shoot, time simply flew by.

I had also bought myself two more dogs, a mother and son, yellow Labradors, the owner had died and his wife was willing to sell them to a good home. She didn't want to split them up which suited me just right, they settled in with Jason well.

Pauline arrived and decided to stop over Christmas, this was good news for the two grandsons and Martyn, the house full of people and Presents building up round the Christmas tree. So Pauline and Tricia were in charge of the house, Mum had her work cut out with the Shoot Party which started to arrive in good time, and of course Barbara Butler was most helpful. Frank also played his part with his tractor and trailer carrying the Beaters around, Colin was more than helpful, he knew his role for the day, our friend John Blackburn turned up so he joined up with Colin for the day. The Boss and his wife went in and saw Barbara and thanked her for the decorations and all the

work she does, "Dare I ask what's for lunch? I can smell," she laughed, "Well, Ted will give you a bit of exercise this morning so hopefully you will work up an appetite."
Colin had his radio so we were in contact with each other, he had made a draw for the pegs, I had already gone with Frank and the Beaters way up over the top. Colin apparently gave the order, "When you're ready gentlemen lets go" one of them was heard to say, "This is great it's like being on a military exercise," and the first Drive they had to scramble to their pegs, so that warmed them up a bit! I still didn't know where a lot of these birds came from. Two Drives over, one to go before lunch and it had to be the thatched cottage and that pleased everybody.

The Turkey roast and Christmas pudding served up by Barbara was a great success, the end of the day was not quite what I expected but was good enough. It was after he had settled up with me, he told me that he had been approached by the "Country Magazine" they would like to do a report by, so we agreed it would have to be a special day so with three Drives in the morning and one good one in the afternoon.
Christmas over, it had been a very hectic time, the Shooting Times were coming the beginning of January that was going to be an exciting day. There were two Drives that we had not touched. I had sorted everything out with Colin so he knew exactly what we were doing, the day went according to plan.
It was at the end of the day when the Boss told me they will not be taking on the Shoot again after this season, because the estate will not be leasing it out again for Shooting, so with one more day to go he advised me to look for another job.
I suppose we should be used to this by now, but that's life in a tied cottage, this meant Colin and Tricia finding

another job and Martyn another school. The bush telegraph worked again: I heard a large estate in North Wales was looking for a head Keeper and Under Keeper. I put this to Colin and he was very interested. I made enquiries and this belonged to a large syndicate. I made an appointment and went for an interview, it did seem a little bit strange interview, he liked the idea of father and son working together. "I'll take you round the estate first, jump in we hardly got in." When he was on the move, hold on! I must admit it was a beautiful and big estate, I thought he was never going to get back to the house, but we did, and what a surprise that was it was a most beautiful house: four bedrooms and one en-suite, carpeted right through, a single bedroom flat adjoined it.

"Mrs Rogers I gather you are a very good cook" "I have been cooking for a number of Shoots" "Well, this is the Shoot Room" Barbara's eyes lit up, I could see she was well pleased, "I think you would like to see the incubator room." This was just across the yard, I had seen one like it before, it will hold, in one go, about four thousand eggs, it was fully automatic, and that there is the laying pen, there are a few left in.

"Now I must tell you, there are three other gentlemen interested in running the Shoot, and want to sell a number of days and this maybe they will want you to take on another young lad," "I would like to talk it over with my son as well," he agreed to this.

I told him I had one Shoot to go, he said he would like to offer me the job and take over the end of January which I agreed, he gave me a number to ring which was his secretary and she will make all the arrangements. We both discussed things on the way home and thought it was a rather strange interview for a job, but I think we were both drawn by the house and by the size of the job, but I was keen to meet the three men who were taking on the Shoot.

I rang the secretary later and she confirmed that we will move on the last Friday in January and meet the three gentlemen on Saturday, but for now I had to concentrate on our last day at Linley which was to be quite a memorable day and we had a good covering of snow, and of course everybody knew this was going to be the last day.
We had a good run through the morning, with three Drives producing a nice bag before lunch, and unbeknown to me the Beaters were out early behind the wall across the road, right opposite the main door way. When the men came from lunch they were as bad as the rest, it was the biggest snowball fight I have ever seen, Barbara and the rest of her helpers watched and cheered from the window, sadly I had to blow my whistle and call a halt. Frank quickly loaded the Beaters on board and went up to Coppice Hollow where I told him to go, Colin stayed with the guns. When finished the one, I could see the hip flasks going round, I could guess everyone was happy!
Then on to the thatched cottage, we collected a bit more ground this time, I don't know whether it was the excitement of the snow fight, or whether celebrating the last day of the Shoot, they certainly emptied some cartridges exactly one hundred and two birds on the day.

Back home, the Boss invited all the Beaters and Barbara and her helpers in to the Shoot room it was like a Christmas party, they all said how sorry they were to be parting company and wished us every success and happiness in the future, the Boss and his wife said they will call round on Monday as we were moving on the Friday. It was a good job Colin had taken the week off and Tricia had finished on Wednesday. Mr Perry and his wife called round and collected what bits and pieces were theirs and settled up with me and Barbara. Friday morning early a lorry arrived, it was between a furniture van and a cattle lorry, I could not believe what I saw, I asked the men who ordered this, the answer was the secretary . We eventually got our home on board we were not happy.

A job Barbara loved doing, collecting the eggs and loading the incubator, then at hatching helping the odd chick out of its shell

Chapter 13

This was to be our eighth move to Corwen

We took the job on so we had to go with it, we had cheered ourselves up by the time we got to Corwen town, the estate was just over the river Dee, we pulled up in the yard, I had hardly got out my car when the man himself came to me "I want you to come with me immediately" I asked him what was the hurry, "He said there's been a fox in the laying runs, but it's gone out now," Well, I said "In that case I've got more important things to do, get my home into the house," he said "I will see you in the morning," I said "Yes, with the other three gentlemen." We took some of the furniture in the house, but left a lot in the conservatory to dry out, I found the heating and turned it on, it very soon warmed the place.
Barbara and Tricia got some food on, we were all pretty hungry and had a hot drink, we were all very tired and stressed out, but did get our heads down after a while.
Colin and I were up early and had our breakfast and talked over what we will have to do first, the estate had been Keepered before by some of the things we saw and found. It was about ten o'clock when a vehicle pulled up at the door and the three men got out. There was one of them who was the spokesman, "Mr. Ted Rogers and this is Colin your son I guess, let me introduce myself and my two colleagues, I'm Mr Rondel, Mr Robson and Mr North, can we have a chat?" "Yes of course, come in, you can see we are in a bit of a mess."
Mr Rondel said "Shall we go in the Shoot Room," he obviously knew his way around, "Now first, we must apologise for what's been a big mix up. The secretary had explained everything to us, now I must tell you what you did not know, I have met your previous employer Mr

Perry and know him quite well, I must say he gave your family a wonderful reference."

"Now we should have been here when you came for an interview, although his Lordship owns the estate, we have the complete Shooting rights and everything that goes with it. That's your house, your wages and vehicle, dog food allowance and pheasant food, but in return we feel to pay for this, we will have to sell a number of days, how do you feel about that?" "Well, I have seen the incubator, which will hatch several thousand eggs but don't know the situation of wild hens, we can catch up." "I see there are some hens in the laying pen here, one other thing we realised, this means a lot of work.

If you feel you could do with another hand you must let us know, Colin what do you think about it? it's obvious you both work well with your Dad," "Yes we get on well together," "We will pay you above the agricultural wage to take in the extra time, now Ted, if you give Mr North your bank account number, you will find your wages will be well above normal. "

"Now Ted can you fetch your wife in we would like to meet her", Barbara was expecting to be included straight away, they apologised for all the inconvenience and immediately said how they had heard about her marvellous lunches and will she be prepared to do the same for them, "Yes I would but, it will be on the same lines as I have done before, which I have to get same help in," they agreed on that and will pay her well when she gives them the bills, but will give her money up front if required.

Well, I think for the moment we have covered most things, but I felt I had to make one thing clear, "Just one thing gentlemen, can you give me your word, that I answer to you and no one else?" They each shook my hand and gave me their word. Mr Robinson, who had not had much to say said, "Ted we don't want you to worry unnecessarily, you answer to us only," Mr Rondel said "Your Land Rover will be delivered in the morning by JS Motors from Corwen."

We all set to and sorted out the furniture with Mum. Colin and myself had to look at the laying pens which were a lot bigger than I imagined, it had a bit of electric fence in places, the twelve Volt battery was flat so I charged that up at home, good job I had a charger. There seemed to be a number of hens and needed a bit of feeding, with the pen fairly safe we had a good look at the incubator room, I looked at it in a different way this time, I opened it, there was still some eggs in the trays also dead chicks, it was going to take a good scrubbing and disinfecting, Colin said it looked as though someone had left in a bit of a hurry.

We were just coming out when his lordship turned up, "What do you think you are doing in here" were his words, I said "Good morning" shut the door and walked away, I was not going to argue with him which I could see that's what he wanted. We were determined to have a good look round and to our surprise, at the back of our house were some sheds which had been set up for the rearing chicks, but had not been used for a very long time and the paddock was for them to have out-door runs when old enough to go out into pens, before releasing into the woods.

It was the first time Colin had had a good look round the estate and was surprised how big it was, his reaction, "I think you will have to think about getting another hand, I can't see the two of us covering this amount of ground," and of course he was quite right, so I said "How do you feel about working alongside another young lad like yourself? I think that's just what we want.

We found some places where we could put up some

catching pens, so we put some food down and the next day he had a bag on his back ready to walk where to put the food out. I carried on looking through the sheds and barns, in one shed there was a heap of electric hen heaters and infrared lamps, in the barn stacks of pen sections but had not been used for a number of years by the state they were in.

Barbara took the opportunity to look over the flat, I phone Mr Rondel and told him what we were doing and what equipment we had found. "He seemed pleased and surprised, I also asked him about taking on a young lad, he said he will leave that up to me, but he will come round to see us next week and have a chat, but to carry on as I felt fit.

The home farm was across the main road from the big house, I phoned the secretary and she said the farm manager would like to meet you, so I made a point of going to see him, John Shaw.

I had not met him before but I guessed the chap I saw in the yard was him, so I introduced myself and asked if he was John Shaw, he said he was, "So you have taken on Keeper's job," "Yes, me and my son Colin and they're willing me to take on another young lad to live in the flat by me," "Crikey! How many birds do they want to release?" "Well, I want to rear and release anything up to five thousand, with a bit of luck I know they want some big days, it's all big money now."

"Well, Ted, I can tell you what my role is, it's to find what beater I can, from the farm hands and a Game cart and a vehicle for the Beaters, but this I haven't done for three years and now it's going to be more of a business and that's where the money comes from selling days Shooting." "John, thanks for having a chat I am sure we will be able to work together."

Every night Barbara and I talked over what we have done during the day, she had already been sorting out the catering side and some of it was a bit of a mess. Martyn had started his new school but was not very impressed, Tricia had found a part time job in a hair dressing salon, Mum was happy to let her do her hair for a bit of pocket money which suited both of them. Pauline rang and told Barbara that her and her husband had parted and he had moved out, but she had kept the two boys.

Barbara suggested that we could do with a holiday, Ted thought for a moment, "Why don't you take the children away somewhere? Colin and I can't possible come," Pauline had told us she had opened a small bank account, so we sent her a cheque and told her we would try and book a caravan at Rhyl up on the coast. Mum will take them all on a holiday, we agreed it will have to be before the end of March, before we start egg collecting. Barbara organised everything. Tricia and Martyn were over the moon to think Pauline was coming again with the two boys, they were lucky to get a caravan at short notice. They were all away the beginning of March, it wasn't the best time of year, but at least it will be a break.

Colin and I had plenty to do catching up hens it meant that we had to visit each catching pen morning and night, but I made sure we had enough, we were catching up a good lot of hens but I was worried the number of foxes there were about. I knew of a taxidermist whose phone number I had kept from previous jobs I had, I told Colin I will show him how we used to do it and if the price was right we will give it a go.

When I phoned him, he was quite pleased because there was not many do that sort of thing now, "I will send you a list of what I could do with" I had several self-locking snares, the ordinary ones had been banned. These could hold them so you could shoot them with a rifle and the skin was not damaged.

We had the price list back which was very good. I found a shed that we could set to one side to only do that in, the skins he wanted were fox, rabbit, squirrel tails, stoat and weasel, so this we could do only when we had time, but the fox was the most important and productive.

Barbara rang and said they were enjoying themselves and plenty for the children to do inside, and the caravan is quite good. Colin and I were busy catching hens, John Shaw told me he seen a number of birds in the spinney leading off from the farm, which was a big help.

We were in the spinney one day. When we heard this terrific siren winding up, I saw John and said "Oh that's his Lordship playing with his prison siren, he will tell you one day. When he wants you, the one you heard was the one for me, but I don't take any notice," I said "Well, here's another one that won't bother!"

Barbara was due back tomorrow so we were not too untidy, the dogs will be pleased to see them, they're not getting too much fuss made of them. It was time for Pauline to catch her coach home, we agreed with her to get the phone connected.

Mr Rondel came round to have a chat, I showed him the equipment we had found and the amount of hens we had caught up, I told him we will want some big netting later on he said "You get what you want because we will want some big days Shooting later on." I told how I had found someone had been in the incubator shed and switched all the plugs on, it was a good job the mains were turned off, I am going to put two bars across the door with two locks, I am pretty sure who is responsible.

The next morning we went to feed the hens, I heard what I thought was a dog whining and sure enough there was a black and white spaniel caught in one of the snares we put down. I took him and put him in the kennels, I had a good idea who it belonged to, yes it was her Ladyship's. She came round that evening and played merry hell, I told her straight "If you let him run loose next time, you may not see him again" I fetched him out, she took it and went chuntering to herself.

I told Barbara we can look for another young lad to come and work with us, she said "Before we went on holiday I found an advert, one was for a lad living close to Liverpool, the other lived just down the road the other side of Corwen", I rang his number and agreed to meet him in town which was a waste of time he never turned up, the other was very keen his mother answered told me he was desperate to get out of town and was very interested in wild life, "Can I have a word with him?" After some interesting questions and answers he said he would like to come for an interview.

Would it be alright it his mother came? She would like to see the flat and she would drive him down. We agreed for him to come down next Saturday morning round about ten o'clock.

Barbara was waiting for them as soon as they arrived she welcomed them, "You have had a long journey," "I'm Margaret Wild and this is my son Michael," "I'm Mrs Rogers, Barbara, and my husband is Ted, he won't be long, would you like a cup of tea?" She knew herself all interviewing we had been through it was all about this taking control for a few hours, "How do you think you would like to live out here Michael? You will have your own flat which is self-contained, it looks as though he has been caught up, but if you like I'm sure your Mum will like to see for herself, so if you follow me it's back out the conservatory, you will have your own entrance," she showed them round, his Mum's reaction was "Oh Michael this is wonderful," "Now I will see you get a hot meal when we have ours and I will do any washing you want done. I think he's just come back, if you're happy, let's go down. Ted, I have shown Mrs Wild and Michael the flat," "Well, what makes you think you would like a Game Keeper job," "I've done some work on the town farm, but I would like to do more," I knew as soon as I shook his hand, it was the sort of grip I like.

"Right Michael I like to take you on, what do you think Colin," they shook hands, "I am sure we will get on okay" he said, "Thank you Mrs rogers," "No" I said "It's Ted and Barbara, we got a lot of work on, when will you like to start," "Can I start Monday?" he looked at his Mum, "I will get him here somehow Monday morning", "Right, I will phone my Boss and let him know I've taken you on from Monday morning, you will get an agricultural wage to start with, but I can see it won't be long before you get the same as Colin."

He looked me in the eye, shook hands with Colin and Barbara, "I won't let you down," I liked that, we saw them walk down the yard, he put his arm round his Mum he was clearly very pleased, they were in the car and waved goodbye. Colin said "Did you see the size of his hands," "Yes, I think he's done a bit of work, he is a big boy for seventeen years", Barbara and Tricia said we like him, Martyn had his say, "Is he coming to live with us?"

Colin and I had gone out early on Monday morning checking some of the snares we had put down and there in one of the three was a "Charlie": that's the name most Keepers affectionately called foxes, although they disliked them for the damage they can do. Colin took the rifle and disposed of him and re-set the snare making sure he put his gloves on, so as not to leave any other smell.

When we got home, Michael had arrived, Barbara made sure he took all his stuff up to the flat. His mother was really pleased with the situation, they were left to sort his room out.

His mother thanked us very much for giving him an opportunity, and Barbara, before she left, told her she was welcome to visit him whenever she wanted, he had his own entrance and his own key, I told him if Colin and I were not about in the morning, Barbara would take him and show him the incubator room. We had already taken out the trays for cleaning so she set him on washing and scrubbing them after showing him, helping the chicks to hatch out was her favourite job, "If you want some more hot water just plug that pot in."

It was nearly lunch time when they came back and they had been out since just after six, Mum said where have you been this morning? Well, we found a small bit of woodland that had some rabbit fencing round I think we can make that into a small release pen, she said "I think it will be best if Michael has his dinner with us each day don't you Ted?" "What do you think Michael?" "Yes thank you very much, I can easily get myself breakfast and tea."

"Right Michael, did you ever think you might be shown how to skin a fox?" "No, I can skin a rabbit. Why skin a fox," "Well, if we get enough skins and feathers together, there will be a bit of extra money, besides your wages. Now there's one thing I must tell you. If you come across his Lordship you take no notice, whatever he asks you or tells you, he is not our Boss, we work for the syndicate".

It had to happen on our way down to the laying pen. There he was, we all said good afternoon politely, "Who's this you got with you?" "This is Michael, he's working with us now I've taken him on," "What do you mean you've taken him on? you can't do that," "Yes I can, if you don't like it you speak to the syndicate." We carried on into the pen to put up some more cover and left him chuntering to himself, "Are these heaps of cover for the hens to lay under?" "That's right, Barbara likes doing that, so she will show you round the pen" "How many hens in here?" "Round about three hundred," "Are they clipped?" "No, we tie the tip of the wing in so we can let out in the wood when we've finished with them, but catching up is beginning to dry up".

I told Barbara she had to take things a bit easier although I knew how she liked to get out and help, I always said some Shoot owners do not realise how much work a Keeper's wife puts in, especially in the rearing season which was rapidly getting close. We all mucked in and finished the cleaning the shelves and put the incubator back together and showed the boys how it worked, Colin had some idea, but Michael had never seen one before.

The most important thing is every egg must be washed, and every time you go out make sure you lock it behind you. We had time to go in the shed and finish skinning the fox we last caught, should have been done a couple of days ago. If the skins had been pegged out to dry you can roll them up together, but if they're wet they need cling film on the west side and then roll them up and parcel them very carefully. We will take these old overalls off, and wash before we go in the house or we'll get kicked out.

Colin, if you will go with Michael in the first shed with sections and start sorting any that want mending, put them on one side, I will go into town and order netting and boards and post these skins off. It's all time consuming, I wonder sometimes is it worth it, but it was good to see Michael having a go and not afraid to get his hands dirty. The rearing sheds at the back of the house had to be cleaned, they were all electric hens, so must get them checked. One day his Lordship was rather polite I wondered what he wanted, "It's my birthday on Saturday and I would like you three to join the Farm Hands, if you go and see John he will tell you all about it." Well, John told us he had got a crackpot idea he wants us to fire the cannons that stand by the front door of the big house, he wants the men to stand behind each tree in the park which rose up the hill where the woodland took over.

I made sure that we three stood well to the side of the park, even then I was not happy that we were completely safe, I could see the party way down the hill at the front door, someone waved a red flag there was an almighty bang, followed with a cloud of smoke with a whistle that I can only imagine was the cannon ball itself which went well up over the top into the wood. He shouted through a megaphone, "Stay where you are," he obviously had primed the other one, a huge bang with a cloud of smoke, but this time it had clearly hit a tree with a big thud, "Party over you can all go now," Michael stood looking rather shocked, he said, "I can't believe what I've just seen, my Mum won't believe me."

Well, we must get cracking on sorting and putting some of the sections up, the electrician had been and checked all the electrics and we have to work out how many gas cylinders we need, it won't be long before they start laying, Barbara's got her egg basket ready.

His Lordship laid in wait for me one morning, "I want you three men to dress the same on the coming Shoot season", "If you mean you want us to have the same new suits, as far as we are concerned you can forget it because we can't afford that," and off he went chuntering to himself.

The boys were working well, together getting some of the sections up, Barbara asked about getting some help with the cooking on Shoot days. I'm just going down through the farm, I might bump into John on the way to the spinney, I was pleased to see a few hens at the self-feeder. We had a big corn bin there so I was able to top the feeder up. On my way back, I spotted John in the wood yard. I approached him on the subject did he know anybody who would like a few hours in the Shoot season helping Barbara with the dinners? "Well, I bet my misses would jump at that, she was made redundant a while ago and particularly did not want a full time job again," "John, tell her to pop up and see Barbara," "Her name is Jill."

Just then there was a shout from across the yard, "What do you want?" I looked at John and winked my eye and shouted back, "I don't want you." "Well, you can keep your eyes off that timber in the corner" which were six sleeper size slabs of oak, I said "What's so special about them," "They're for my coffin," "Well, if they're put together, you will want a crane to lower them into the ground", off he went to his office chuntering away to himself.

John said "I will tell Jill to come up and meet Barbara." On my way back I spotted Barbara down the end of the yard looking at the laying pen, I could see what was in her mind. I waited until she turned so as not to make her jump, "Oh where have you been? the boys have gone off I was left on my own.

Colin has taken his gun and Michael took a spade", she said "Let's have a look in the pen, the birds are fairly quiet now they have got used to us feeding them," we had a slow walk round a few hens tucking themselves under a bit of cover but not sitting tight so left them for today and agreed she would look round tomorrow.

"Let's go back to the house and have a cup of tea, if Colin's taken his gun he's seen something he wants to get rid of," I sat down on the settee and found myself dozing off, she sat down with me ask "What are you thinking about?" "Well, Wally has just crossed my mind," "You haven't mentioned your brother lately," she held my hand, she knew we were very close to each other, she held my hand and snuggled up to me, we must have dropped off because we suddenly woke up, I looked at the clock, "Blimey! It's four o'clock," I tried not to wake her but she slowly woke up, "Are the boys back? Oh look! We never had our cup of tea, let's have one now then I'll take the dogs up the field for a run".

I saw the boys coming across the hill, if I cut across I can meet them at the bottom, they both seemed pleased with themselves, "Well, what you have been up to?" Colin said, "I didn't tell at dinner time, when I went round topping my self-feeders and Michael done his, I spotted a black cat, I knew it was up to no good the way it was. It could only be a feral cat, so I thought I would give Michael a bit of experience.

I hoped it was still about this afternoon. We were close to where I saw it, we crept on a bit further, we both suddenly froze, there it was having a good meal. I put my fingers to my lips, Michael nodded, I was trying to work out whether I could get a clear shot, there was a lot of rubbish between us, I slipped two cartridges in.

Suddenly it moved but it didn't run off, it obviously had a mate, I was up quick, killed one and the other one went down but not killed, I put one cartridge in, put the gun in Michaels hand, go and finish it off, I wanted to see if he would do it. He had no hesitation, he dragged it back it was a pair, was I glad to see them dead, they could have done no end of damage to us, we dug out a hole and buried them".

What a good afternoon they had I praised them well, a good job done, I asked Michael if he would like his own Gun, he said his Mum told him she would get him one.

I said to the boys, I think we will put another infra-red lamp in the huts with the electric hens, you can help me do that today. Mum wants to look round the laying pen, I wouldn't be surprised if she found a few eggs. I saw her out of the incubator shed with her basket. We gradually got all rearing equipment ready for chicks which would not be long.

His Lordship had been in touch with the syndicate and told them he wanted us three to have new suits and we will have to go and be measured and fitted, I said "There's no way we got time for that," so he agreed we went to a Tailor's in Corwen town and got them off the peg, but that was after they had had a big row which I was not going to get into. Mr Randle came and found us and persuaded us to go and get them at our convenience, but he wasn't satisfied with that, "I want you to put your suits on and come and stand at the front door of the big house and have photographs taken with me," I said "No way, we're not your puppets, we will only wear them on Shoot days," but when we got home, I asked Michael to put his on and come in and we will put ours on and let Barbara inspect us, I must admit, they were plus two's and felt quite good, she said "You look very smart."

Barbara was collecting a nice few eggs, I let Michael go with her twice a day to collect, he had never seen anything like it, Barbara explained to him, when you find a clutch of eggs, you mark one to leave and take the rest and they will lay to that one, but you've got to keep your eyes open, because they will tuck in anywhere to lay. Colin spent most of his time washing and cleaning ready for me to pack them in the incubator trays each one numbered and dated, the machine switched on the blades spinning round to keep a constant air flow, I will explain the trays will turn twice in twenty four hours.

When we got another batch ready, we will fill some more trays, and water trays must be kept filled to keep the humidity up and the process went on and on until the seventeenth of May, we had our first hatch, so outcome the first trays of chicks on the bench where Barbara was in charge.

There was a few did not make it out of the shell, there was enough chicks to go into one of the sheds with the electric hen and infrared lamps. Michael helped me put them in the shed, he was quite excited, the other two carried on their tidying up and cleaning the trays for me to fill up again and start all over again. This went on for several weeks until all the sheds were full, we all knew we were going to be very busy.

I told the boys we will each have our own beat and release pen, but would help each other when needed. Mr Rondell arrived one morning just as we were getting the last hatch out, there was four trays to get out, "Can I help." "You can, if you would like to help Barbara box some up, we will take them out to the last houses." The boys and myself were flat out back and forth getting them under gas heaters, I heard Barbara say "Gather them up in both hands, Mr Rondell, you won't hurt them," and was I glad to see the last lot go out.

Barbara suggested we clean ourselves up and then come up for a cup of tea, I asked Mr Rondell if he would like to have a look round and see what we got, he jumped at that, "I would very much," we went to the big sheds first, he was quite surprised to see how many there was, these look lively enough and you've got those other smaller huts full, that's marvellous, "How many do you think you will release?" "Well, you said you want some good days, I would like to think we will put out about five thousand," "Well, I think you've all done a wonderful job, if I can put around about that figure, we will be well, pleased." I suppose I can put up with his Lordship for a bit longer, "Ted, I know how you feel, but we'll talk about that later in the season and Barbara, I will look forwards to your dinners on Shoot days," she said "I have been able to find someone to help me," "Oh before I go, your still able to go and collect what food you need from the stores in Corwen?" "Yes I will do that." "Now the next time I see you I expect most of the birds will out to the woods, I shall be away for a while but any emergency you have my consent to deal with it, I will give you my card to cover that."

Well, that was a surprise visit! I didn't expect to see him, I'm glad he's given us the go ahead because it's going to cost a fair amount altogether, well I had better tidy up the incubator shed and put the machine to bed, who knows what next year will bring, we must keep an eye on any feather pecking. I think I'll go and get another de-beaker, I'm sure we won't get away without doing it. Sure enough Colin spotted one or two having a little peck, so we quickly set to with Michael catching, Colin and I de-beaking, Barbara brought out a drink, it looks like you could do with another hand, "I knew you could not resist helping" because she had helped me do it so many time before. We quickly got going, she showed Michael how to catch and hand them the right way to Colin which made it easier for him. Barbara said "I will give you half an hour and then I will go and get some food on, no one's had any dinner today" "Right we will do this house and have quick look round and we will be in."

The dogs always had to be involved in, even when we were de-beaking, they will sit for hours just watching, knowing they dare not touch them, it took us nearly three weeks to get through. It was time to give each house a little bit more room outside and then they started to grow with exercise, and the food was going fast as well. With that job done Michael asked "What are we going to do with the laying hens?" "Well, I have always put them to the woods, but this year we will catch them up, cut the tap of their wings and they will soon get the use back, in fact some may still want to lay and hatch off, if they do it will be a bonus." "Colin, you know what to do, if you and Michael find some wire, make sure you make a funnel big enough, feed them as usual and don't forget to whistle and the chicks as well, they will connect with the food."

I went down to the farm and had another chat with John Shaw, he was pleased to think his wife Jill was going to help Barbara on Shoot days, he asked how the rearing was going, he could not believe when I told him how many we were hoping to put to the woods. I said that's our next big job, he said "I don't suppose you could do with another pair of hands," "Why what have you got in mind John?" "Well, I still got a week's holiday to take I would not mind giving you a hand," "I'll take you up on that John, I'm sure we can come up with some arrangement," "Well, I've been left my Dad's shot gun, I got a licence, I thought I might take up a bit of clay Shooting," "Say no more, Colin has done quite a bit of that, he hasn't had much time since he's been here and Michael is keen on getting his own gun, I used to do quite a bit myself but it got a bit expensive for me."

I think we will start putting the birds to the wood on Monday early, John said "I'll have a few days off then," we had started to cut the heating down a bit so they well out into the runs and harden off a bit. So the three of us made a last inspection of all the pens and the electric fence round each one was working, the dogs had a good run out, I said we'll have a couple of easy days apart from feeding.

We were all up early, we had put the crates ready, Tricia was home that week, Martyn was home from school it wasn't long before we had the first load ready to go. John and I took them, Barbara and the two boys caught up, Tricia and Martyn opened the catch so they could pop in the birds quickly and close them. John told me he had never had much to do with the Shoot before so he was very surprised to see what we had going, he said "It was never a big thing as far as he can remember," "Well, this year the syndicate has made a big business of it, they will be selling days' worth several thousand pounds a day."

I made sure we were able to get to the gate of the pen easy and made wide enough, we quickly got them in and undone the catches to let them find their own way out, that did not take long. We loaded the empty crates back on and went down to get another load and before we looked it was lunch time, we'll take this lot and then just fill six more crates out of the other house and that will be enough for this pen.

We arrived at the pen only to see his Lordship there he shouted at John, "What are you doing helping him? you're not paid for that," "I will do what I want when I'm on holiday" John retorted, we took no notice of him and just carried on and back for the last lot safely taken to the wood, it was nice to see some of the first ones out were already feeding and drinking and hopping up onto the lower twigs and branches.

Back at the yard, Jill, like John, had never been involved with Shooting or Keepering before, so was really interested. Barbara as usual had been back at the house and put the good old soup pot on she called out to Colin, "If you got time for a break, bring everyone in" this was something different for Jill and John, she had already set the table, Jill asked can I help? "Yes please, if you pass the bowls to me," "Barbara this smells delicious," we sat round and had a good old chat.

"Barbara can I have your recipe?" Colin laughed, "I think that's a well-kept secret, plus a good old cottage loaf," "Help yourselves to a slice of bread, a can of beer and a glass of wine for the ladies," Tricia said "Mum this is like the old days we used to have," Ted said "We got another three days before we get them all to the wood," Jill said "I can contribute to the next three days," Barbara said "If you can come a bit earlier I might let you into a little secret." The next three days were hectic with all the poults in three pens, Barbara called us in for another meal and Jill let slip that she helped Barbara make the soup, but still did not know the secret ingredient, but did promise her that when in the future, if we left she will give her the secret .

"Well, boys, it's time we checked the pens. Top up the feeders and spread some food on the ground" John asked if he could come, "Yes of course, I will drop you and Michael off at the first pen, we will go on to do the other and pick you up on the way back and go on to the other pen because that's the other side of the wood." John noticed we had a number of big oil drums for corn bins, he asked me if we could do with more, "Yes I could," "Well, I got some at the farm you can have they want cleaning out," "That won't be a problem, we can do that with the pressure washer at the farm, when you come to pick them up I will show you the Beaters' cart, they haven't been out of the shed for years."

I told the boys we will do as much hand feeding as possible this will mean a lot more walking and carrying of feed bags, I said I will do the middle pen and all around it, Michael chose the one to the right, so Colin agreed to do the furthest one away, he liked the area. The birds were growing well, and coming to the whistle, although they had funnels to get back to the pens, we realised there was that many outside, we had to open up some of the ride ways and feed them up, it was good to see hundreds of them spread out on the feed.

It was getting to the end of September when Barbara took a call from Mr Rondell, saying the three of them will be calling in about half past ten tomorrow morning. This was a chance for the boys to show off all the work they had done, we fed early and back for breakfast, I said "I will finish off taking the big nets while I am waiting for them to come, you go and start knocking out where you think you want another feed ride." Barbara had the kettle on for tea or coffee, she welcomed them in and they had a biscuit and coffee, "I'll give Ted a shout, he's out the back taking the nets off the runs."

I heard her calling and answered her back, after untangling myself, they're not the easiest thing to fold up on your own, I washed my hands and went in, they instantly jumped up and shook my hand, "Well, how's things been going Ted," "Well, we've put a few out to wood" Barbara could not hold back, "A few?" she giggled and turned away laughing, so I said to the gentlemen, "Perhaps the best thing will be is for you to jump in my Land Rover and I can take and show you what we have been doing."

I drove quietly up to the pen where Michael was waiting, we got out, I introduced them to him, he was very polite and shook hands, good morning sir to each one, "Gentlemen, if you come with me, Mike will go and feed" I took them onto a slight bank where they could see both rides. With his bag on his shoulder he went off whistling and straight away birds were coming from everywhere, "My god! What a sight! Well, I don't think I've seen anything quite like that."

Right if you jump in, I went to Colin's pen, as if they had planned it between them, he was waiting with the same idea, they got out, Colin was halfway down feeding whistling the same tune, he knew I wanted him to come to my pen later, the look on their faces, they were truly excited what they saw.

Right one more stop, Colin jumped in the back we stopped on the main ride, he got out and started whistling. The birds they were all round us, but he walked off down the

ride, "Well, Ted what a sight, well, what sort of bag will you be happy with Ted?" "At least two hundred and fifty to three hundred birds, so if we said we want ten days Shooting, well, I am sure we can cope, but I must see how Barbara feels, I have no doubt she will go along with that." Mr North said "There's no time like the present," he asked if I thought she will be about now while we're here, I am sure we will find her doing something. Back in the yard, she had the dogs out giving them a good combing and brushing down, I called her to come in, "We're sorry to interrupt your dog grooming Barbara, I'll know where to bring mine. Now, Barbara we have just had a most wonderful sight, we never expected to see so many birds, now Ted sees no reason why we could not have ten days shooting and how do you feel about all the cooking? It may be a day in the week, most of the guests Shooting will be foreign," "Well, it won't be foreign cooking, it will always be good English roast dinners'," "That's good enough for us, and of course your special Keeper's soup we have heard about and you can get some help," "Yes I have already organised that." "Barbara, we will give you a lump sum up front and top it up as we go on, is that alright?" "Yes thank you."
I said "I have had a chat with John Shaw and he's looking forward to it," "Yes I meant to have told you we arranged costs with the agent, I don't want you to worry about that.

Now can I give you the first date? It will be the last Saturday in October and they will be American's," "Oh I will look forward to them, I have heard stories about foreign Shooting," "Well, some of them don't know what organised Shoots are like, but we want you to do the draw for the pegs and we will make sure they have plenty of cartridges." "I think I told you I planned for five Drives, three in the morning and two in the afternoon and we will help pick up, my dog men will keep well back to start with. Barbara will be in if anyone would like a cup of soup." "Now if you like I can let Colin take you to each stand," "Yes I think that's a very good idea Ted," Barbara asked John and Jill Shaw if they will stay behind after to have a drink and a bite to eat.

We were feeding fairly heavy now as the birds were begging to spread out across the woods, with a week to go after feeding one morning, we carried the pegs with us and pegged out, well, I could not resist the first Drive had to be way up the park, right in sight of the big house the three of us stood at a peg each.

What a beautiful sight that was, the two boys looked at each other and commented, this is going to cause some excitement.

"Now Michael, your job will be to help keep the Beaters in line and no shouting or whistling, there will be no dogs in the line, just keep tapping your sticks, John will know where to bring the truck to take the Beaters to the next Drive and you will know where that is because I will work with you."

Saturday morning came we had to be out and feed early , we met up and walked back for breakfast, Barbara called Mike in to have his with us, Tricia went in and turned the heating and the lights on in the Shoot Room. "Colin, I will have Jason with me today, you concentrate of the team of guns. I knew the dog will behave with me.

Three vehicles turned up in the yard, it was the syndicate, I went out to greet them, they were obviously feeling good between them, then suddenly the yard was flooded with vehicles, they were ushered into the Shoot Room With all the introductions over. Barbara and Jill were ready with the soup, this was something quite unusual to some of them, but the reaction from most was of really pleased, Barbara and Mr Rondell, he caught her eye and put his thumb in the air and gave her a smile, he then said "Gentlemen I would like you to listen to our head Keeper for a moment." "First I would like you to take your peg number and each Drive you move up to, Colin will lead you to the Drive pegs, please listen to him, at the end of each Drive I will blow my whistle, Mr Rondell will also accompany you." Suddenly one of them, "May I ask," "Yes of course," "Are we allowed a loader?" "Yes I gather some of you have someone with you for that, well, have a good day gentlemen."

Give us fifteen minutes Colin, I quickly caught up with the Beaters. I looked back, I saw Colin at the bottom of the park, under my breath I thought, hang on Colin ten minutes, I need not have worried, John let us all off quietly, Michael did his job we lined out and started steady and slowly, was the word down the line, the Shooting was continuous it seemed a long time before we got anywhere near the end but I had my whistle ready. I did get a glimpse through the trees and there was birds falling everywhere, so we pulled out. I blew the whistle quickly, Michael collected the Beaters all on the trailer and we were back at the top ready and waiting round the end of the big wood, this was just right for them to walk back to the yard and get what vehicles they wanted for the last Drive before lunch.

Colin told me the second Drive was more testing for the birds and the guns, they had to weave their way through the tall trees and on towards the guns, they asked for more cartridges, Mr Lownds said "Yes", we have a short walk back to the vehicles in the yard and we have a wagon which will take us to the last Drive before lunch, this wagon is one that John fetched out and made it very comfortable. This was driven by another Farm Hand. Colin rode with him to make sure they parked out of the way.

Michael was on the end of the line, so he could see if some of the end guns were on their pegs, he sent the word down the line to start slowly, by the sound of the Shooting there were a lot of birds going out, I looked at my watch not quite half an hour to go to lunch. By the time they collected their selves together and the chatting had died down, they climbed onto the wagon and home for lunch.

Barbara and Jill were waiting, they liked the idea of the soup, Tricia made sure who wanted soup. Meanwhile Barbara was putting the lunch together, Jill had the plates on the hot trolley, it was a good old fashioned beef roast with all the veg you could think of and finished off with a mixed fruit crumble and custard and they could help themselves to the bottles of wine on the table.

No one noticed, but his Lordship walked in, "I would like a lunch please," Barbara was flabbergasted, she looked across to Mr Randell, he nodded his head as if to say all right, he was heard to say, "You have killed too many," one of the men said "We have had a magnificent morning and we have got the afternoon to look forward to." Barbara asked if anyone would like a second helping of pudding, well, there was three of them could not resist.

Colin thought some of them were getting too comfortable, he had a quiet word with Mr Rondell, he smiled, give them twenty minutes and then have a word Colin.

Colin was trying to be polite, "Gentlemen I'm sorry to disturb you, we have twenty minutes to get ready and onto the wagon, no rush," as they went out, they all thanked Barbara for a wonderful lunch, I had got the Beaters going as we had a fair way to go. I knew Colin would be in position by the time we had lined out. I had a quick word with Michael, he said, "Ted I never imagined a day's Shooting would be so exciting," I told him not to be surprised if they ask to clean their guns at the end of the day, but Colin will put you right on that, I had already put the gun cleaning kit ready for him.

We were well, on our way down, birds were flying well, and a lot of Shooting, the picker up men had hung the mornings kill in the cool room, I blew the whistle for the end of the Drive, I wasn't worried about this Drive, I knew the last Drive would be a good one, I wanted this one to be very slow. I knew Barbara and Jill would be busy and Martyn and Tricia would be helping to clear away the dishes and tidy up again. I didn't take Jason with me in the afternoon, Martyn fed the dogs before we got home.

The Drive ended the Shooting party huddled together at their wagon, the Beaters had already gone home, we waited for the dog men to finish their picking up, eventually we got into convoy and made our way back to the yard with the birds hung up and counted, three hundred and five, someone asked if there was anyone to clean the guns, Colin's name was quickly put forward He told them to lay their guns in their sleeves on the table in the conservatory.

He and Michael set to, it didn't take long, and when they came in they brought with them a wide range of drinks, Barbara had put out a number of plates full of sandwiches which went down very well, Mr Rondell asked me to call them to order and announce the bag, there was a terrific round of applause and the drink was quickly going round. I heard the figure going round, one of them jumped up and asked for a toast to the wonderful lady who served up the lunch.

The three syndicate men came and shook my hand, you certainly hit the jackpot, well, I certainly didn't do it on my own, Barbara and family played a part, yes we want to see her before we go, he shook her hand and placed a generous wad of notes in her hand, "Barbara, can you produce the same again next Saturday? "Yes I will certainly do my best," he called Colin and Michael over and thanked them for all their work and gave them each a cheque.

The rest of the party was moving, each one collected their guns and shook Colin's hand and left a note in it, John and Jill stayed for a bite to eat and a drink with all of us, they never stopped talking about the day. I had paid the dog men, the Beaters will be paid by the estate but I felt I had to give John something for all his help, at first he would not take it, but after telling him I want his help the rest of the season he accepted it, Barbara had worked Jill's money out and gave her , you will find a bit extra, she gave Barbara a hug and she said I have enjoyed every minute of it, I was pleased for Barbara , she had made a friend.

I am glad they didn't have far to go, ten minutes, and they would be home, I could see Michael was ready for bed, I reminded him to feed his pen in the morning not to wait for me or Colin, we went into the lounge and collapsed into each other's arms.

The freezer lorry came on Monday morning, birds loaded, that was all sorted by the syndicate, Jill came up to see if she could help clear up and help in general, "Well, would you like to help Tricia to clean up the Shoot room?" the men came back from feeding just right for coffee, we still had the heating and equipment to clean and put away and pen sections to take down and put in sheds.

The week went by, and we had been feeding the spinney at the farm with the help of John, this was to be our first Drive, the party had arrived, Barbara and Jill went through the same process, this group were used to this way of English Shooting, they knew how things went. John took the Beaters well, round to the bottom of the spiny, Colin waited for the wagon in the farm yard before walking into position. This turned out to be a much better Drive than expected, once again we moved into another new Drive, but this one was a bit disappointing, but I knew we could move to another which would be busy and would push the bag well up.

With a few various birds, there was two hundred and thirty pheasants, six woodcock and eight partridge, I asked where the partridge came from, John told me he had seen them on the field close to the wood. End of the day.

Lunch time had been really enjoyable, according to Mr Rondell this day was more in his line. They put their guns straight in their vehicles, they didn't want them cleaned but they enjoyed the soup and sandwiches and thanked Barbara generously.

The syndicate had a word before they went, "Ted, do you think you could incorporate us in with the guns? We would like to have a day's Shooting," "Well, I don't see why not, have you got a full team this next week?" "Yes, but we have got to give them priority," "Well, how about if you stood as back guns? Because I know some of the Drives a good number of birds curl back over, Colin can take the main team, and you come with the Beaters, I will let Michael take you to your pegs I think you will be alright," "Well, that sounds alright, it could be exciting."

I saw John in the week and planned everything as best we could. Barbara and Jill were well, prepared for the lunches as they were for the rest of the days up to Christmas, this day went well, and everyone was well, pleased.

The last days Shoot before Christmas was close, the syndicate said they would like a really special day, they'd obviously taken a lot of money up to now, I told them they could if they accept there's only two days Shoot for after Christmas was reasonable.

They asked to see Barbara and asked her if she could put on a Christmas banquet for a few children as well, as their wives, she smiled, a proper old Christmas party, "Will that be the last Saturday before Christmas," He looked at the others, they were in full agreement, I must add to this, it will be a Shoot for our own guests.

They gave Barbara the money they owed her and a nice bundle up front, "Barbara, make sure you give me the bill for everything and I will pop round the Friday before." They shook hands and thanked the boys for their personal help, especially taking the guns to their pegs and such like. "We will see you all at Christmas," they were in their vehicles and away.

It had been a very busy day for all of us, Barbara had made a nice drink, Michael didn't have much time on his own, only when he went to bed. We were just relaxing, the phone rang, Tricia said "I'll get it," she was very excited, "it's Pauline," they had a quick chat then handed over to Mum, they chatted away, the outcome was, "Can we come up for Christmas,?" "You know you can come any time," "Well, I've booked on a coach that's coming up to Rhyle and can drop me off right off right outside the Drive to the estate, I've had the phone on now for a fortnight, I will call later and give you the time we will arrive roughly."

Well, can you believe that! It looks like we will be going to have a house full, Jill is coming up in the morning to help tidy up, and so we needn't worry about it tonight.

We had a fortnight to feed heavily and get the birds back, Barbara had a chat with Jill and asked if they had nothing booked for that Saturday would her and John like to spend the day with us as well as helping, I also had a chat with John because I relied on him, I told the boys we will do the same Drives we did on the first day.

One evening I could see Michael had something on his mind, he didn't really want to go to his room like normally, Barbara nodded her head to me, so I said "What's on your mind Michael, is something wrong?"

"Oh no," he sort of stuttered, "Well, I was wondering if my Mum could come on Saturday and stay over Christmas," poor lad he had a tear in his eye, immediately Barbara put her arm round him, he obviously missed his Mum, "Of course she can she will be more than welcome. In fact it would be better if she came on Friday."
"Thank you Barbara, can I give her a ring in the morning?" "Yes when you come back from feeding."
Michael was so pleased to ask his Mum down for Christmas, she had only been a couple of times, so it all going to be a pretty exciting.

Martyn asked if it was going to be the same as we had at the last place, Tricia said "No it's going to be a lot bigger," "Can we have a tree this year," "I will see what I can do". I said to the boys, let's see if we can finish getting the rearing equipment in this week, then next week we will take thing a bit easy, but we've got to keep the feed going and we will re-peg the Drives.

We were all set for the last week before the Shoot, Jill came up every day and was thrilled to bits that she could help, and she went with Barbara to the butchers and other shops. Pauline rang to say she will be arriving about two thirty on Thursday, so she will help with the finishing touches to the decorations all round, plus the tree.

Everyone seemed to be coming on Thursday, Margaret was first to come, Michael could not wait to show his Mum round in the Shoot Room, "Barbara, I have brought a few things with me, if there is anything I can help with, please tell me," "Well, this is Jill my help mate, but tomorrow we will be very busy," Tricia asked "Is it time to go down to meet Pauline?" "Yes but be careful keep off the road." Ted called the boys, "let's go and feed, Jill are you and John here for tea tonight? He did say he might come," "Well in that case, we will be here," "Will you and

Margaret set the big table up in the lounge, please? You had better set for ten of us."

Suddenly the door burst open, were hear Nanny and straight into Barbara's arms, "Where's Grandad," "He's had to go and do some work he won't be long before he's back.

Barbara as usual ready for anything, we all sat down to a good hot dinner and a lot of chatting, Jill told Barbara to sit there I will go and get the pudding, Margaret jumped up let me help. Pauline and Tricia cleared the dinner plates, Barbara said everything must be washed and cleared away tonight, tomorrow will be another day. Dinner over, we all sat down and had a good chat, John said "It's going to be a big day tomorrow Ted," "Yes I hope it will be."

Pauline had put the grandchildren to bed, Colin told me he had put the dogs to bed, Margaret laughed, "Do you put them to bed as well," "Oh yes but we wouldn't use ours tomorrow, do you remember Michael how the first day went," "Yes I do." John and Jill said their goodbyes and see you early in the morning.

Michael and his Mum retired to his flat, Pauline asked if she could have a talk, what news you have got to tell us, "Well, I got my divorce a while ago and I hope I have found a completely different person, Jenny has been very kind looking after the boys and letting me have a bit of time to enjoy myself at last, his name is Andy Robbins, I first met him playing darts which he is very good at.

I met his Mum and Dad and got on very well, with them, I have put my name down for a council house, so fingers crossed. When I go back, he has promised to meet me at the coach station, he worked all the times out for me so I should be alright."

"Well, I am pleased you have told us we do worry about all of you, at the moment we have tomorrow to think about and we'll have another chat before you go home, now let's go to bed."

All up early next morning and ready for breakfast, that finished and cleared away, Barbara had her soup saucepan ready and dishes on the table.

A land Rover pulled in the yard and out jumped the syndicate, another one was behind and out jumped the wives and children it was going to be a day out for them. Mr Rondell led them all in, Tricia asked how many would like a bowl of soup, the word had got round how good it was, in no time at all the rest of the guests arrived.

They all had to be called together and go through the same routine as before with Colin in charge of the guns, today John had already gone with the Beaters but this time the syndicate would take a peg each.

Three Drives in the morning, I spotted Colin each time we came out, I could tell by the chatting it was a good morning again they were able to walk back through the yard and to the Shoot Room.

The table was already laid with Christmas crackers for the children and turkey meat of the day with all the veg you could think of and then of course the good old pudding with custard, Barbara had organised her helpers to make sure everybody had what they wanted and of course his Lordship turned up and had his lunch.

Mr Rondell and his wife found Barbara in the kitchen, "Barbara we really must thank you for the marvellous lunch and Christmas tree and decorations," "Well, there will be sandwiches and cake when you finish," "I honestly don't know how you do it," "Well, I have my helpers, if you want to leave the children this afternoon, Pauline and Tricia can keep them occupied with some Games and singing," "Oh that would be absolutely marvellous."

Again John had gone with the Beaters

The team of guns followed in the wagon and got out

quietly with Colin in command. It wasn't long before the Shooting started, I knew it was going to be a good day, we eventually went onto the last Drive, I had thoughts in my head about looking for another job remembering what Mr Rondell said a long time ago.

The day ended on a good note, the picker up's done a good job, back in the Shoot Room, the table had been laid with plates of food, but covered over with cloths. Barbara came in, "Who's hungry" taking off the cloths.

The party got underway and the music for the children, suddenly Colin came in, "Just one minute, I am sure you would like to know the bag for the day was three hundred and six," a loud whoopee and everybody was enjoying their selves, Mr Rondell came to me , "Ted, I would like a word before I go," I took him into our lounge, "Well, Ted it's been a fantastic day, I know you have not been completely happy here," "Well, I must tell you I will be looking for something else," "This is why I want this word, please don't look any further, I can honestly tell you I have a job lined up for you and Colin," "What about Michael?" "Well, he always said if ever he left here his ambition would be to work in a large zoo with animals of birds."

"But we have two more days shooting," "Will you have a word with Michael," "Yes I will, now just one other thing, I must tell you we are giving up the Shoot and sell everything up. Ted, I will come and see you after Christmas and tell you more, let's get back to the party," Barbara came to me, "I wondered where you had gone," the grandchildren were all mixing with the others.

Mrs Robson, Mrs North and Mrs Rondell all came to Barbara and thanked her individually for a wonderful time she had provided for everybody, Mr Rondell had already settled up with her and me. All good things must come to an end called one of the Mums and lined them all up to

thank us, which we thought was very nice. John and Jill had gone home, but told Barbara she would be up in the morning to help clear up, we all had something to eat and drink and sat talking.
Barbara looked at me and knew I had something on my mind and came and sat beside me, Margaret looked a bit out of her depth, Barbara said "I think I know what's on Ted's mind, I've been through it all before," "Well, I might as well, tell you I had a chat with Mr Rondell this evening and he told me they were not taking on the Shoot again after this season and would be selling up everything.

I told him a long time ago that I will be looking for something else, he asked me then not to be too hasty but wait until after Christmas and it was now he had something lined up for myself and Colin, Michael you will not get the sack, I know he will do all he can to help you find another job," "Well, there's a place nearer to home which I would like to work on," "Well, we have two more Shoot days, but if you feel you would like to go back with your Mum for a few days and have a look round, I will give you a reference and Mr Rondell will be calling round next week."
It's been a hell of a season and I don't want to take on another as big as this, he and his Mum went off to his room, Barbara looked at me, "I think there's a little bit more to it than that," "Well, it's a friend of Mr Rondell where he gets an invite to Shoot, his Keeper will be leaving at the end of the season, it's a single handed, but is also looking for a maintenance man who will take over when the time comes for the other man to retire, all I can tell you it's on a small estate close to Stafford England and I won't know any more until next week." Pauline said "Oh good it will be close for me," Colin said "He used to like building work," Tricia asked "How about me, but I

don't think we will be sorry to move." Martyn said "I will be glad to go," Barbara had her say, "It's been a big experience for us all, but let's all agree we will be behind Dad whatever he chooses to do."

Right we must remember we got two more Shoot days, the freezer lorry called the next morning to pick up the Game which was Sunday, they pick up whenever they can.

The three of us was out early to feed, Michael asked me if he could go back with his Mum tomorrow, Monday, he's got an idea he might have the chance of a job at the place he used to go. Pauline was getting ready to go home Tuesday morning, I took her to Corwen to catch her coach, it was dead on time, "You will let me know what you're doing?" "Yes we will" and saw them safely in their seat and waved.

Mr Rondell came round to tell me more, the Charnes Estate is owned by a gentleman who always wishes to be known as JH and Mr John by his workforce, he would like you to ring his office at the Charnes estate the last week of January for an interview, it's a small village called Wetwood in Staffordshire, I will be Shooting there next week so I will have a chat, but I will be back for our next day, these will be continental team of guns.

I asked John to come up one evening, Jill liked coming to see us, she rang and told Barbara they will be up that evening. Colin and me were busy without Michael, John and Jill came in and we sat having a drink, "Well, John I've got some bad news for you, we will be leaving at the end of the season," Jill cried "Oh no, you can't" she held Barbara's hand "Is this true,?" I'm afraid it is, well, they're not keeping the Shoot on again so it will mean we will have to move, but we have found another job on a small estate back in England near Stafford with the help from Mr Rondell."

"John, don't forget we got a Shoot this next Saturday we will have to take in some outside ground for these next two days," and Barbara asked Jill for her help, "Of course I will." Michael came back on Thursday morning and he could not wait to tell me he got the job that he went for, his Mum turned straight round and went back she said I will come and pick him up last week in January.

Mr Rondell called in the middle of the week it was about lunch time and Barbara asked if he would like a drink and something to eat, "Well, that will save me stopping on the way home," "Ted, take Mr Rondell into the lounge, I am sure you will find something to chat about." Lunch will be in ten minutes and no sooner said it when she called us in, my word it certainly smells good, we sat down, "Now Barbara are you sure you have got enough money,?" "Yes I've already got Saturday lunch sorted, I will give you the bill for that next week," "Do the boys not come in for lunch," "Yes they do, but something is holding them up, I never worry too much, I can rely on Colin," it was just then the boys came back, "Michael I'm very pleased you have found another job, I have written you a reference" and handed him an envelope, and "Ted, you ring that number to make an appointment for that interview, well, I will see you on Saturday morning."

Colin again took charge organising the guns, I went out early with John and the Beaters to take a bit more ground, first Drive went well, second Drive not quite so good, I found Colin and told him to move the Drive which will take in his pen that pushed the bag back up and back for lunch. Barbara was a bit surprised there were no ladies today. That made lunch time a bit easier, she made sure the Beaters had their cups soup.

Lunch over, we set off for two good Drives in the afternoon, with all the birds collected and hung in the Game cart, we made our way back home with another two hundred and seventy two birds to add to the tally, everybody was well pleased.

The syndicate thanked Barbara and settled their account, they said how sorry they were to lose the Shoot, "Next Saturday, Ted if you think you can fit us three in again we would like to," "Yes, no problem I think I might have a surprise for you," John and Jill stayed again for tea before going home.

After feeding round early, back for breakfast, I asked the boy to go down the farm to fill some bags with corn so we can top up the self-feeders and big barrels, we won't have to worry about them. Before we finish we will hand feed up to the last day's Shoot.

Later that morning I rang the estate office saying who I was, the secretary said "Mr Rondell had spoken to the Boss about the vacancy for Game Keeper and your son Estate Handyman, he instructed me to make a time and date for an interview, "now will Wednesday the last week of January at ten thirty be alright,?" "Yes, that will be perfect," she said "I will put you in the diary and look forward to seeing you all."

I came off the phone and told Barbara it's a good job we keep all our boxes for packing, and that's two days before our last Shoot, Michael said he would like to help that day and can his Mum come the day after and take him back?

I rang Mr Rondell and told him what Michael wanted to do, he said he would get his money together and pay him off on Saturday. We had to be up early that Wednesday morning, we wasn't sure how long it would take us, but Jill said she would come up and keep Tricia and Martyn company.

We arrived at Wetwood cross roads and saw The Hall marked up, we were a bit early and took our time going up the Drive and there was the sign, Estate Office very impressive.

I parked the car and walked across a gravel yard, she must have been looking out for us, just as I rang the bell the door opened, "Good morning, Mr and Mrs Rogers and Colin, please come in, I'm Margaret the secretary, the Boss is on his way," the door opened he walked in, "I feel I know you all, Ted Barbara and Colin,"

The maid came in with a tray of tea and biscuits, Margaret poured the tea "Help yourself, well, I hear you have had a very hectic season."

"Yes it's been nonstop from start to now and we've still got one day to go," "How many have you released? It was just five thousand," "Good gracious me! How did you manage that?" "Well, we could not have done it without Colin and another lad," "And Barbara you have cooked for all these people."

"Well, I did have some help and must admit I don't think I want to do it again" I butted in "And I certainly don't want another job like that again," "Well, I have had nothing else but praise from Mr Rondell," "Well, they gave me their full support," "If I offered you this job and said we don't want any more than two thousand, and it's a completely private Shoot and sadly Barbara there won't be anything for you," "Oh I always find something to do," "The hatching is with oil heaters," "I will be quite happy with them."

"Now Colin we come to you, I understand you have done some building work," "Yes I done three years with a chap who had his one man building business bricklaying, plastering and plumbing, I can do all that." Now Barbara, "I think it's only fair to let you see the house," "Yes I would like to see the house," "Right if we get in the Land Rover, I will run you round to have a look and then back to the house."

We turned off the road into a small Drive in the corner of

a field and there was the house, "Now, we are doing some alterations, Colin I want to introduce you to Cyril who does our building work," he asked Cyril how long before he will finish, "I will be finished by Friday," "Come in and have a look Barbara." A nice big kitchen, two small rooms, because we had a big sitting room where we are, I could see what was going through her mind, "now Barbara what do you think," she said, "Well, there's only one fireplace at that end so was this one big room once," "Yes it was, are you thinking you would like it back to a big lounge again," "Well, it would be much better for us," he looked at Cyril, "What do you think Cyril?" "It will be no problem because it's not a load bearing wall, its only wood and plasterboard," "Right we will get straight on with that Cyril," "Yes but there will be some decorating to do," "Well, we have an account with a firm in Market Drayton, if you will do the decorating we will pay for the materials," "Oh that will be alright," she said, "Ted, what do you think?" "That sounds okay with me."

"Right, let's get back to the office" Margaret had a cup of tea ready quickly, "Well, Ted I would like to offer you the vacancy" "Well, thank you very much Mr John," "And Colin, I would like to take you on as handy man to Cyril and your wages will be paid every Friday by Margaret." "You say you have a Shoot this Saturday and you will finish the following Friday? Margaret will you book a furniture removals for Wednesday that week and confirm that with a phone call to Ted and Barbara? I believe you have another boy and girl?" "Yes there's Tricia and Martyn she will be looking for a job, but Martyn he has another six months at school." We shook hands, Margaret handed me an envelope and said I think this will cover your expenses, he came to the door and wished me luck on Saturday, "See you in two weeks" and waved us goodbye.

We stopped for a bite to eat, back in the car and still chatting over the new job, arriving home just right for tea. Tricia and Martyn could not wait to hear all about it, Jill had just gone home but will be back in the morning to help prepare for the Shoot dinner, Barbara as always had that well in hand, I was sorry in a way. I know she was going to miss all that, but was glad she wasn't going to have that worry every week, she could get back in her garden which she loved doing and there is a big garden where we are going.

Michael was back, so I told the boys what I had planned, we will squeeze in four Drives in the morning. We will do the first one across the road behind the farm, with three syndicate wanting to Shoot, I have pegged them forty yards behind the line, in between the guns. Colin you do the draw as normal, I will have a word with Mr Rondell, I will tell him what we are doing and Michael you help me with the Beaters same as before, I have put John right so he will know what to do. So if you go round together tomorrow, Colin, if you stand Michael on one peg and stand on one behind, you will see how it will work.

I asked Barbara if there was any last minute items she wanted, no she was quite happy, I have planned for six extra, he hasn't said how many there will be, we were alone in the kitchen she said "We are going to miss all this hustle and bustle" and gave me a kiss, "Yes but we're still together" and gave me a big hug, I said "You know what, I've just had a thought," "What's going through your mind now?" "Well, with all our moving around the country, I would recon it would make a good book," "I don't think so," "Well, I could tell someone who might be interested." She danced around singing `Teddy is going to write a book`, Tricia came in what's all the fuss about? Can I join in, "Dad's going to write a book, I hope it will be a best seller we will all be rich", with that we pulled ourselves together and got back to being busy again.

Saturday morning came, one Land Rover turned up with the three syndicate men, I made my way to meet them, I wanted to make sure that they knew exactly what the plan was for them to be back guns.

They had heard of that before, but never been asked to do it, they were quite ready to try it out, knowing Colin would be in charge. The rest of the party turned up so we all made our way into the house, soup was on the go if anyone wanted it, Colin quickly made the draw, knowing I had already gone with John and the Beaters.

Mr Rondell had found Barbara and said how they were looking forward to something different today, she knew what he was talking about, because I had already told her, "Well, I hope you have a good day," They were on the wagon down through the farm and quietly on to their pegs. John had put himself in site of the guns so he gave me a signal they were ready, we didn't hang about, we had four Drives to do this morning. We certainly had pulled the birds there, with our feeding the Shooting was very brisk, the three extra guns made a big difference. When we pulled out Mr Rondell had his two friends with him, they had some good birds in their bag.

We moved to the Park Drives where they had walked up to their pegs with their backs to the big house. John had the vehicles ready for to move on each time, the last Drive over before lunch But today they got a lift back home, we were running a bit late, but things were going smoothly, Barbara and Jill had the lunch ready for them, again perfect timing.

Two Drives in the afternoon wasn't going to be easy for the spare guns, but I did manage to fit them in some open spaces but they would have to be quick, but after they told me how exciting it was.

Day over back home, the syndicate thanked John and the pickers up for all their help, two hundred and eighty five birds, and many thanks for Barbara, all round.

When everyone had gone, Mr Rondell, Mr North and Mr Robson came to see us as a family, they said how glad they were we had got the job in Staffordshire and wished us the very best in the future. He asked Barbara if she would pack anything belonging to the Shoot, leave it in the conservatory and he will come round before we leave and pick it up. He paid her up to date, we had, over a few weeks, been packing things into boxes and bags we were just about used to it by now.

Mr Rondell came round on Monday and picked the bits and pieces up, I asked him to have a look and see how we had collected all rearing gear up. All the gas bottles had been taken away, I made sure I had locked the sheds up and gave him the keys.

A lorry came on Tuesday evening and loaded some of the furniture on, now that's what I call a furniture lorry, some difference to the one that brought us here, it even had a place for the dogs. Jill and John came in the morning as we were putting the last on, Jill and Barbara said goodbye and promised to keep in touch, once again we were on our way.

Looking thoughtful,
Ted planning the next day's Shoot at Wetwood

Chapter 14

Ninth move to Wetwood Staffordshire

I knew this was our ninth move Keepering on our own again, we arrived at Keeper Cottage just after twelve Cyril was there tidying up outside, it had all been altered inside so we quickly set too and got unloaded, Barbara and Tricia sorted the kitchen out, Colin and I moved the furniture around, cups of tea were very soon coming.

The lorry men had a cuppa and was soon on their way, Cyril came in for a chat, he left two decorating books which we could choose from up to a certain price. "So do you start with me on Monday then Colin?" "So I've been told," "Well, our workshop is across the main road, where you turned off," "Yes, I saw it when the Boss showed us round."

It was quite a big garden which Barbara was pleased with. She was going to have more time on her hands, but I know she will be out with me at some times, and getting the house sorted. But once again my first job was to look round to see how many hens I could catch up, the laying pens was in good condition and incubators were in a shed in the garden, but the rearing sheds were up at the farm at the estate yard, no gas bottles all electric hens, each shed had its own outside big runs.

Tricia found herself a job, but she was still set on hair dressing, she bought herself a motor bike this helped her to go as far as Market Drayton and Newport and was well pleased. Martyn went to his new school and was much happier. We kept in touch with our friends, Tricia's god parents John and Dori Blackburn, they told us that they had gone out of Keepering and bought themselves a fishing shop down West Country, he was always keen on fishing. I phoned my brother and sister-in-law before we left, she told me Wally had not been well, I said I will ring again when we get settled in. I gave her my phone number, but didn't wait for her to ring, I rang her, she said he had been taken into hospital that morning but will keep me informed.

I came back from the woods one morning, Barbara was stood at the gate waiting for me and burst into tears, "Peggy rang just now, Wally died yesterday." We went in the house and both cried, him and me were very close. We gradually pulled ourselves together and sat down and talked. Wally's son Steven rang and told us when the funeral will be, I saw the Boss and asked for a couple of days off, he agreed I should go.

It won't be long before I start collecting eggs so I made sure there was plenty of food in the self-feeders for the hens. It was quite a while since we saw Nell and Reg and when we told them we were moving close to Stafford they immediately wanted to come and visit us.

We left to come home straight after the funeral so we were home the next day. I was surprised, when Nell and Reg arrived, to see her in a wheelchair. After greeting them, we learnt she had been ill and determined she was still going to get around so they sold the Caravanett and bought a bigger one, perfect to Drive her wheelchair up ramps and big enough for a bed and a toilet, and cooking facilities.

The days were going by quickly, I had started collecting eggs and Barbara found it a bit strange not having anything like we had at the last place, but being on my own, I had plenty to do. The incubators were working okay. Once I had a number of chicks, I had to take them in my car up to the farm where the rearing sheds were. I eventually got a small tractor with a box on the back which was a big help, Barbara loved driving that around. Colin started going to night school to learn a bit more and get his certificate.

Our first hatching over, poults were growing well, with one release pen in the middle of the estate and a small one up a valley on one side of the estate. I could see the amount of Shooting days was going to be a lot less because it was a private Shoot and invited guests, we knew this was going to lower our income quite a lot and we had adjust to that. The pheasant poults were growing and will soon be going to wood, I also had to check over the duck Hides which needed a bit of attention but they won't be wanted until later in the season.

Martyn was going to school still but was looking forwards to leaving. He had been going to a local farm which his friend's parents owned and did get a job there when he left school. Tricia was still hair dressing, Trevor was working and living in Milton Keynes.

It was time the birds went to wood, the pens were ready and Colin said "If you do it on Saturday I can give you a hand" and of course that went for Martyn and Tricia. I always said a single-handed Game Keeper would not be able to do the work they are expected to do without help of the family and a lot of Shoots take it for granted that he will cope one way or another. I must say I have been very lucky with my family, I hope I have been able to reward them somehow at different times. And so the birds were collected and put to wood, and now I was on my own again feeding constantly, Barbara of course helped when she could and at last got the house how she wanted.

The Boss came down and was pleased the way we had decorated the house and started on the garden and growing a lot of our own vegetables. Barbara loved the garden and coming round the woods with me and the dogs. It was getting close to the first Shoot, eight days were booked by the Boss four of them will have an evening duck Shoot.

The first Shoot was the end of October. We had agreed which Drives we were going to do so I had pegged them out, the guests had met at the big house. The Boss made the draw himself, the Beaters mainly came from the farm workers, one picker up, Ray Williams, who was a regular in the past and Colin worked with him with one of our dogs.

The guns and Beaters met at my house, Keepers Cottage, and I was introduced to the guests and who should one be, none other than Mr Rondell! the Boss said "I don't think this gentleman needs any introduction!" was I pleased to see him, and he never stopped shaking my hand, he asked if he had time to see Mrs Rogers, "Yes of course we won't be moving off for ten minutes" "Ted, do you want to take the beater on? I will blow my whistle when we're ready" They only had to go across the field to their pegs. Barbara told me later, how pleased he was to see her and wished us all the very best.

I knew this was going to be a very different Shoot than we had been used to, smaller Drives, more time spent in between Drives with the guns having a chat and of course a tipple. Lunch time came, the Boss took his guests back to the big house and Beaters back to Keepers Cottage where Barbara was waiting with her big pot of soup, the big shed I had got ready before hand for the Beaters.

They had all got comfortable and soup went down very well, but it was time for me to shout them all to their feet and off to the first Drive after lunch. It looked as though they were all pleased with the morning's Shooting. While we were waiting, Colin said to me, "This is a bit different, Dad, to what we have experienced in the past," suddenly the whistle went and we were going through some very rough woodland. It was the sort of Drive where the birds didn't have a good opportunity to get really high, but the guns were experienced enough to only take the highest ones, it seemed strange not to have the two boys helping me.

We pulled out and the Boss came to me and remarked how well that went, he asked have we got time for one more Ted, I said we certainly have. Colin had already gone with the Beaters, as far as he was concerned it was all in a day's work, I know he did like being involved with Shooting, live pigeon Shooting or clay Shooting.

By the time I caught up with them, I heard the Boss's whistle go and we were on our way with the last Drive, the birds collected and loaded in and hung cart drawn by a magnificent shire horse back to Keepers Cottage, no convoy of four-by-fours on this Shoot.

The Boss came to me, "Ted, will you sort out a brace for each gun and bring up to the front door at the Hall in about an hour?" Colin and I picked out some good birds and laid them in the boot of my car. I didn't have long to wait at the door, they gradually emerged out saying their goodbyes to their host and coming to me with a good old fashioned hand shake and discreetly passing a tip in doing so and taking the birds and thanking me for a good day. Mr Rondell was the last one out and thanked me generously, I had the feeling this might be the last time I would see him.

Colin and Ray had hung the birds in the cold room ready for the lorry next day. Tricia and Martyn had done their bit during the day, three more Shoot days went by, another year without a holiday which brought us up to Christmas. The Boss told me he always liked a Boxing Day walk round, he will ask two or three of his friends, and would I like to invite some of mine who helped out? "We will have lunch out, Ted, if you can find a nice spot." This was no problem there was plenty of pit holes and boundary spinneys which I asked if they could be pulled together with some pheasant cover to help out with the main Shoot days, but he didn't want to do that. There was a derelict old building in a pit hole I had marked out to stop for lunch, I had dropped off some straw bales beforehand and surprisingly we all made ourselves comfortable and of course Barbara had made sure we took some of her famous homemade soup and to add to the lunch, the Boss handed round a couple of his favourite tipple Sloe gin.

Time to move on and gradually walked our way back to Keeper's Cottage, the Boss took what birds they wanted and back to The Hall. The rest of us sat down in the shed where Barbara had kept the tin fire going for us to use. We all had our own stories to tell, we booked one another to help out to end the Shoot season. We had one more Shoot day and then a cock bird-only day which most of these men will come to again, but a bit more organised, and that was Christmas over and the end of another season gone and Barbara said and one more without a proper holiday.

It was then that I made up my mind we were going to have a holiday. We agreed to go for a cottage, luckily she picked one that someone had cancelled at the last minute, Farm Holiday Cottage up country in the Lake District, and she booked it straight away for the last week in March. We rang Pauline, she was only too pleased to come up, I told the Boss I would like the last week in March off, he asked "Who is going to look after the hens we have caught up?" I told him he need not worry, the family will look after everything that I'm responsible for, his answer was "I suppose you had better take the week off then."

Another Shoot season gone, we left the family to look after things while we were away, and Barbara and I were on our way up the M6, we stopped at Gretna Green just right to see a wedding at the famous Blacksmith's shop, quite a special sight and tourist attraction. We turned off at Carlisle down a windy country lane, Barbara said "Are you sure we are on the right road?" I laughed and said "I hope so" and straight away dropped into the farm yard and on the gate post a board saying Cosy Farm Welcome to the best bed and breakfast and holiday cottage in Cumbria`.

We had a great welcome by two friendly Collie dogs and quickly followed by the farmer's wife Mrs Anderson, "Will you follow me out of the gate and round the back of the farm?" and there was the most beautiful narrow driveway which I did not see and a lovely converted farm building into a Bungalow.

We were quickly out of the car and greeted each other properly, "My name is June" "and we are Ted and Barbara," she said "I'm sure you would like a cup of tea, I will show you inside" and there was a table laid with cups and a kettle to be switched on, milk and sugar and a lovely homemade cake waiting to be cut. "Now I will leave you to settle in and I'll call round later".

We had had our tea and put our clothes away and just settled down and having a chat when a knock on the door, yes it was June and her husband William. We asked then in, we had a drink and a good chat especially when he knew I was a Game Keeper, the evening went by quickly, as she left, she told us if there's anything we needed we'd only got to ask and take a jug to the dairy and someone will fill it.

And so we carried on with our holiday, we didn't venture far, mainly took a nice picnic with us and a bottle of wine out on the moors. Tucked in behind a stone wall in our chairs, soft music playing in the car and talked a lot and promised ourselves we'd have more holidays in future.

But all good things came to an end, reluctantly we packed up and thanked June and William for a lovely holiday in a beautiful setting and said our goodbyes, and so made our way home to a happy family.

Colin had started collecting eggs with the help of the girls, Martyn fitted in helping with the dogs and rotavating the garden, we very soon got the incubator going. Barbara loved it when they started to hatch out and her fingers itching to help those few out that could not make it. She boxed them up and I had already been up to the farm and set the electric hens going.

Pauline was ready to make her way back home with the two grandsons, we took her to the station where she caught a coach, Tricia was always sad to see her go and they thought a lot of each other, but she had her motor bike and she liked doing hairdressing.

The chicks were hatching well, and soon had around two thousand in the rearing sheds, the Boss was quite pleased with what he saw. I carried on repairing release pens. Wherever I was working Barbara would bring the dogs for a run, she would also give me a hand especially with the netting.

The other pen was at the far end of the estate, this was a job that had to be done each year, falling branches was the problem also badgers digging under the wire until we got the electric fence going.

The Boss told me he did not want to shoot the ducks this coming season so that saved me another job not having to rebuild the duck Hides.

Barbara liked to watch Colin clay shooting so she drove him round different Shooting grounds, Martyn was into his tractor driving, JCB and bigger machines, Tricia still doing her hairdressing and riding her motor bike everywhere.

The birds were just coming up for releasing to pens in the

woods and spotted one shed had started feather pecking, without fail this meant de-beaking. To do this each bird had to be caught and with an electric iron you cut the tip off the top beak, it doesn't hurt them or stop them feeding, it stops them pinching out feathers off other birds.

Barbara was an expert at catching them and handing them to me to do the job. This was an early morning job we could well have done without. By doing it, it stopped it spreading and we lost no birds.

The next two weekend was taken up releasing them all to pens in the woods again, this was done with the help of the family crating then up and a tractor and trailer from the farm. I set them up with feeders and water troughs and barrels spread around the woods kept topped up with corn. As I walked round, I could fill up a bag on my back and spread by hand down the rides and open spaces, I was glad to see them starting to go up to roost.

It was coming up to our twenty fifth wedding anniversary so we had a little party before the Shoot season started, this was another excuse for Pauline to come up again for the week. Colin was going to evening Building classes to learn a bit more, where he met another lad Russell and met his wife Lily and also became good friends. Barbara's Mum and Dad came down from Yorkshire for a couple of days. Party over, the Shoot days were upon us before we knew it, but as always we coped with it very well, and the Boss was pleased also.

Christmas came and went, Boxing Day walk around and one day's Shooting in January to finish the season I started catching up the hens for the next year coming, Barbara had talked about having a holiday but we never seemed to get round to it, so we made sure we got out and about a bit more and done a bit more shopping.

Pauline came up with the boys in the summer and told us

that her and Andy were getting together more and next year might be their big year, and we had not met him yet but had spoken to him on the phone quite a lot.

Colin was well into his Plumbing and Building, he had also met up with a young girl, name was Joy and looked lovely, Trevor was married and living in Milton Keynes and doing what he was always keen on, being a mobile Mechanic, Martyn was happy working on a local farm tractor driving.

We did not have a lot of contact with the Boss, he just popped in to see how thing were going, and I made a point of taking him round some feeding times so he could see the birds.

Tricia was still hairdressing but was talking to Barbara she would like to get into a bigger shop to get more experience. Trevor turned up unexpected with his wife Kim for a few days and two grandchildren. Kim over heard what Tricia said and jokingly said 'come down to Milton Keynes where there is some bigger hairdressing salons looking for younger people' and of course Tricia was more than interested.

"Mum can I do that?" "Where will you live?" Kim said "You can come and live us," "Oh I think you ought to take your time and think about it." Well, she was old enough to make up her own mind, and so that's what she decided to do and off she went to Milton Keynes to live with Trevor and Kim and found herself a new job hair dressing which was just what she wanted. And Christmas over and another year gone by.

A few hens caught up, I had a phone call from the office to see the Boss, this was the end of February thinking he wanted to talk over the coming season, but it came as a complete shock when he blurted out, "I think it's time we parted company," so I hit back "Where do you think I'm going to get another Keeper's job this time of year?" "Oh you will" he said, "I said you give me the sack then," "Oh, can't do that," "No, because you haven't got a leg to stand on," I said "I've had it up to here with tied cottages so if you want me out find me a Council house," "I'll see what I can do," and I walked out completely ignoring him.

I went home and told Barbara, she completely broke down, the next day I went and let out what birds I had caught up.

A person who lives on the estate I knew quite well, came to see me, and offered me a key to a council house to go and look at in a village called Seighford near Stafford

This was our garden at Wetwood Staffordshire

This is our front garden at Seighford.

Barbara loved seeing the fish in the pond

We had never had neighbours in all the houses and jobs we had until now, it was in a Close of twenty houses

Chapter 15

Is this going to be our last move to Seighford?

It didn't take long for us to go and have a look, but we soon realised it was going to be different, set in a close with neighbours houses all round, but there was a little shop and post office, a school a pub and a church, but you could say it was set in the middle of another country estate, but a number of houses had been sold off and we somehow liked the idea of living there. Three bedrooms, small garden back and front the two boys were happy with it, although Colin told us that he and Joy were getting married so he would be getting a house on the estate where he was already working. Tricia found herself a new job hairdressing which was just what she wanted.

The new house was empty, the old lady had moved out two or three weeks ago. On returning home with the key I was told if we wanted the house to keep the key and clean it up and move in at our convenience. Two weeks on, we had moved in and settled with the rent and the house was ours and somehow we felt free, but then we had to find work. We already asked for the telephone to be fitted and that was coming next day. We made a number of calls, we had some return calls, some never bothered, one offered a Warrener's job. I wanted to be more than a rabbit catcher. Some said you're too old, this made Barbara cross, she wrote a letter to the Shooting times saying 'too old at fifty' which was published.

I was sorting out my tools and traps, Barbara tapped me on the shoulder, "Why don't you start your own business?" I said "Don't be silly we haven't got a clue," this was in the morning. We had dinner, I carried on outside for a bit, Barbara called me in for a cup of tea, "What do you think of this?" she had scribbled on a bit of paper "Stafford Pest Control wasps and vermin control", "I will put this in the paper and I will do all the paper work and any accounts that have to be done," she laughed and said "I will be your secretary."

Well, I just had to go along with the idea, she had already been in touch with a firm in Yorkshire and they were willing to send down a batch of stuff, accompanied with a travelling sales man. By the end of the week I was surprised how many calls we had although there were a few pest control firms in the area. I soon realised I could answer a call in the same or next day, that's what the customer wanted and keep the cost down when I heard what some of them were charging and a big help from Barbara being able to Drive.

I noticed she was started to favour one leg and this meant a visit to the doctor and to the hospital for x-rays, and after a while she had a hip replacement which was very successful and soon back to normal.

Martyn had found himself a young lady and they moved into a flat in the town, but he was a country lad and soon found themselves moving to a cottage on a farm which they rented off a local estate close by us and then they got married at the local church.

I was approached by the local estate to do some work, Pest Control, fencing, and tree planting and the like, Martyn was also able to help me out to earn himself a bit extra money. Tricia also rang and said she had met someone and would like to bring him up to meet us and were planning to get married, It suddenly dawned on us how quickly the family had grown up and flown the nest, but we were always a close family and kept in touch with each other.

Barbara and I had decided it was time we had another holiday and agreed Ireland was the place we would like to go. She already had a holiday brochure and picked out some cottages, one I liked was in Galway, northwest Ireland, most were already booked up but we were in luck because they had a late cancellation and that fitted in with the ferry crossing.

Barbara was very busy the next few weeks on the phone, it seemed a bit strange working for ourselves up to a point, how and when we worked, but we could not afford to turn any work down. It planned out about four weeks to go before we went on holiday. We got the work up together and packed our bags and was on our way to Scotland to catch the ferry from Ciarnyan across to Larne, Northern Ireland, we drove across some lovely countryside and enjoyed talking to the local people as we went along, but did not realise we went over the border into Southern Ireland but this did not cause any problem.

We went as far as the coast and found a little village called Billy Beg and asked in a little post office if they knew where a cottage called Nut Meg Cottage was, and in a lovely Irish accent "About five minutes down the road standing on its own with a board on the gate "Nut Meg Cottage".

A young man was mowing the lawn, he ran to open the gate and welcomed us in, "I'm Brian, mother told me to be here and meet Mr and Mrs Rogers and she will meet you tomorrow," he gave us the keys and showed us in, told us where everything was and quickly got our things from the car had the kettle on, we soon settled in and went to bed.

We had already agreed not to travel around too much but relax and take things easy, we were sat out next morning when the woman who owned the place came round, it was Mrs Owen, and she said "Sorry I was not here to meet you" but hoped her son looked after us well.

Thinking back, it wasn't long after we moved to

Seighford, I was asked to join the village committee, they already had a project in mind to improve the Village Hall and this was going to need a lot of money, John Al——ss was running a lottery, Tony C—e doing a Fish and Chip evenings and some other bits and pieces, but I felt it wanted something bigger. So with the help of Barbara and family he organised the village Fete and made various table Games, this was done for a few years and in time, the money was raised for the hall to be modernised but sadly, unlike the village Ted was born in all those years ago, the village life was not like it used to be down in Sussex .

We had been sitting out and going through our life, where and what we had done, the day was coming to an end and ready to go to bed and sadly the weeks holiday came to an end and we had the same way back as we came. In the car park at Larne, Barbara got out to stretch her legs, but somehow Barbara lost her footing and tripped over, hearing her cry out I realised she had seriously hurt herself, I quickly attracted the attention of the security and between them and the ferry crew got us parked on board and made as comfortable as possible .

We were well on our way across when a member of the crew came and said they could see Barbara was in lot of pain and were prepared to get a helicopter and lift her to a mainland hospital if she would agree. I knew she would not agree, all she wanted was to get home to Stafford. On reaching the harbour the ferry crew were wonderful getting her off and into the car.

To this day, I will never know how I drove all that way down the M6 to home. The ambulance came and she went to hospital, on visiting her I had a feeling something wasn't quite right with her, but having had her hip replacement she came home.

I carried on working with some help, time went on and Barbara was getting about a bit more and asking questions which did not seem to make sense sometimes.
The last Fete came and we got through it, Barbara tried to get round the best she could. When it finished the family agreed with me I was not going to do another one. Sadly no one in the village was willing to take it on.

One day she had a fall, insisting she was alright but I knew she wasn't, the following morning coming down stairs two steps from the bottom she tripped and fell hitting her head on the front door, this was another hospital visit. Sadly she was not well enough to come home and we had to find a care home as a respite for her.

Abby Fields then became her new home, I went in every day from 8am till 5pm, while I was in there I gave her breakfast lunch and tea. I was practically part of the furniture, and was well known by the patients and staff, helping out wherever I could.
I promised Barbara I would keep the garden going and I did.
After falling ill with a chest infection she was admitted to hospital. After a short stay I decided to try and care for her at home. This proved to be harder than I thought and after another fall the doctor said she was suffering memory loss and the start of dementia. This meant she needed constant care, so, with a heavy heart she was move back to the care home.
After 5years of being well cared for, Abbey Fields was sold, and all dementia patient had to find alternative accommodation.
Finally Barbara was given a room at Rose Villa Nursing Home as her condition had worsened and needed 24hour care.

I still went in every day as before, gradually eating and drinking became virtually impossible.
Barbara was admitted to hospital again, as she became unresponsive I was told to contact the family, we all knew how ill she was, and after two days in hospital Barbara passed away peacefully with me holding her hand.

It was January 13th 2016, two days before her 83rd birthday

That's all for now---Ted.

Printed in Great Britain
by Amazon